M000249852

3.22

CARING FOR MILLIONS

*For my wife Marjan and my son Julian who encouraged
and supported me in writing this book.*

&

For my parents.

SUMMIT PUBLICATIONS

ISBN: 978-1-7352100-0-1 (print)
ISBN: 978-1-7352100-1-8 (ebook)

Ordering Information:
Special discounts are available on quantity purchases by corporations, associations, and others. For details, contact summitpublications@captiva8.com

Contents

CARING FOR MILLIONS

Secrets to Starting and Building a
Successful Home Care Business

K A M R A N   N A S S E R

CHAPTER 1

By Way of Introduction

There is no place like home.

The sentiment was true for Judy Garland's character, Dorothy Gale, in the classic 1939 movie *The Wizard of Oz,* and it applies to millions of seniors who struggle with their daily tasks.

By 2034, for the first time in United States history, the country's elderly population is expected to surpass the number of children.[1] The graying of America, as some call it, will primarily be driven by the 73 million–strong baby boomer generation that is turning 65 at an astonishing rate of 10,000 individuals per day!

Our aging population is requiring more care than ever before, a trend that's set to explode during the 2020s and 2030s.

The demand for home care services, in which caregivers help seniors with their daily nonmedical needs, has never been greater. Home care is a vital, challenging, exciting, and rewarding industry—and it might be the perfect career field for you.

If you're thinking about starting a home care agency or you want to supercharge your company's success, this book is for you. In it, I will share what I wish I knew when I started my home care company in 2013 in California with less than $20,000 and a dream.

Choosing home care

I was drawn to the market opportunity as well as to the desire to help older people and their families. There's a feel-good aspect of the home care industry, something that's missing in many other business opportunities.

But I had little knowledge when I entered this field. I didn't know where or how to hire quality and reliable caregivers, how to train them, how to find clients, or how to run other aspects of the business.

Succeeding with hard work

It took lots of humility, effort, determination, and grit—but by 2017, my company was named (at number 206) to the *Inc.* magazine list of 500 Fastest Growing Private Companies in America, with a three-year growth of 2,103 percent.

The company was also ranked number three in the *Silicon Valley Business Journal*'s list of fastest-growing companies in Silicon Valley and number 13 in the *San Francisco Business Times*' list of fastest-growing companies in the Bay Area.

I was so proud of my dedicated management team and our achievement when the business was honored, particularly since there are so many other great technology firms and businesses that are heavily funded by venture capitalists in the San Francisco Bay Area. We were expanding more rapidly than companies that had raised hundreds of millions of dollars. That was a monumental achievement, which not only showed we were doing something right but also hinted at the enormous market opportunity ahead.

With the meteoric growth of the business, several larger companies became interested in acquiring us, and in 2018, I decided to make a successful exit, which allowed me to pursue other endeavors.

Those endeavors include my new company, CAPTIVA8, which helps home care agencies connect with potential customers through a customer engagement platform. Consisting of a 24/7 online chat tool and app, the platform reduces the time needed for agencies to match their caregivers with potential clients—from a matter of days to a matter of minutes.

I developed the idea of CAPTIVA8 while I was running my agency and used it to capture and engage with potential customers. The idea worked, and we tested and refined the process further, after which we decided to make it a standalone product and bring it to other agencies.

The decision to pursue home care for your loved ones is a heavy responsibility. CAPTIVA8 provides an efficient and effective method to match customers' needs with an agency's caregivers, providing peace of mind while streamlining efforts to generate leads.

Starting your home care journey

My experience has showed me how difficult it is to enter the home care industry—and how rewarding it is to see your company succeed.

Think of this book as a curated collection of publicly available information, insights, and resources, all saving you from having to sort through a ton of data. As you establish your own home care company or endeavor to grow an existing agency at a faster pace, you can use this book as a guide. Chapter 2 offers a broad look at the senior care industry, while chapter 3 highlights the different types of home care agencies. Independently owned agencies require fewer startup costs but more planning and effort to grow. Franchises come with higher initial costs but an easier path to stability.

Home care is a chicken-and-egg kind of business, featuring a balance between hiring and training caregivers and matching them with customers. If you don't have customers, the caregivers will find work with other agencies. Without a mix of caregivers, you'll struggle to land customers.

This process repeats for months—sometimes longer. You have to keep at it, to continue hiring and training caregivers and advertising and marketing and finding potential customers.

It's exhausting. But if you persevere, you'll land a few clients and you'll have the perfect caregivers for them, and then you'll start building income and confidence. Once you get the ball rolling, you can keep repeating the process, and the ball will roll faster and faster and the company will become easier to operate—your "flywheel" of success. That flywheel is fueled by marketing (chapter 5). Marketing is everything—the difference between your company's success and failure. We will discuss your company's flywheel model in depth in chapter 6. While your patients are your company's central focus, covered in chapter 7, caregivers also require attention and care, a topic that's addressed in chapter 8. In chapter 9, we take a look at innovation, new ideas, and the future of home care.

Caring for millions

The home care industry will experience both opportunities and challenges in the coming years, and we need to be ready as they emerge. The next few decades will see us **Caring for Millions** of aging Americans—and they deserve the best care possible.

Here is my perspective on how you can help seniors live healthier, more fulfilling lives while you guide your company to new heights. Because there's no place like home, and there's no industry quite like home care.

CHAPTER 2

The Industry and Why It Matters to You

It's time to get inspired by what you do!

Maybe your current job isn't cutting it. You pour your heart into your work, day after day, and the days bleed into months and the months become years, and eventually you wake up and don't feel the emotional connection to your job that you used to.

That's what happened to me, anyway. I worked in the publishing industry before I made the switch. I spent eight-to-ten hours a day designing magazines. My work got printed and shipped, and after all my effort, most people threw the magazine in the trash. And then it was on to the next magazine.

I was good at my job. But over time, I became dissatisfied. The publishing industry was changing. Circulation was declining and advertising rates decreasing, and there was a lot of anxiety about the future. So, I started considering different options. What was I going to do with my life? What would I find fulfilling?

After months of research, home care came onto my radar. I thought it was an interesting option, and the more I looked into it, the more I liked it. You can make good money running a home care agency, but money isn't the motivator here. Money won't fuel your company's success—enthusiasm and a sense of purpose will. With home care, you work directly with people who need your help as you strive to improve their lives.

True motivation

If you can find a career that makes you happy, satisfies you emotionally, and allows you to live comfortably, there's nothing better.

As I started my new career, the day-to-day feedback from patients' families and friends and from hospitals and nurses made me excited to wake up early the next morning and start making calls and dealing with cases. Some of the cases were extremely difficult. But I wanted to figure them out and help clients thrive.

In the home-care business, you might handle cases involving drug-addicted family caregivers providing inadequate care to their elderly parents, leaving the parents in dire need of food and medication management. Complicated cases could involve law enforcement and fractured family dynamics. And it's up to you to navigate these different components and turn the situation around.

It's deeply satisfying when you can help somebody. You don't get that feeling in every job, but it comes with home care.

Enter the home care industry because it inspires you. The earning potential, while significant, is secondary.

Home care boom

The leading growth industry of the 2020s isn't centered around computers, manufacturing, banking, or oil and gas. It's home health care services, a sector that includes non-medical home care, home health care, and hospice. The U.S. Bureau of Labor Statistics predicts four percent compounded yearly growth in the home health care services sector between 2018 and 2028, for a total increase of nearly 50 percent—more growth than in any other industry.[2] That sector is made up of a number of different areas of care:

- Home care, which involves nonmedical private-duty agencies providing non-skilled care. Caregivers help clients with Activities of Daily Living (ADLs), such as eating, bathing, dressing, toileting, and mobility. They also assist with Instrumental Activities of Daily Living (IADLs), including cooking and medication management. There are an estimated 26,000 home care agencies in the United States, which each generate about $1.8 million in average annual revenue, meaning the industry brings in roughly $47 billion per year. About one-third of the agencies are franchise operations, and the rest are independently operated and affiliated agencies. The costs of home care are not covered by Medicare.

- Home health care involves agencies that provide skilled nursing care (which is covered by Medicare) by registered nurses (RNs) or licensed vocational nurses (LVNs). Home health care RNs and LVNs provide services such as taking vitals, giving injections, treating wounds, administering medications, providing physical and occupational therapy, and managing prescriptions. Nearly 12,000 home health care agencies operate in the United States, and home health care is estimated to be a $44 billion industry.

- Hospice care, involves palliative or end-of-life care. Hospice workers assist terminally ill patients with pain and comfort management, oversee medications, and communicate with the patient, their family, and other stakeholders. There are about 13,000 hospice agencies in the United States, which generate $25 billion annually.

Combined spending for home care, home health care, and hospice care topped $100 billion nationally for the first time in 2018 and climbed to nearly $109 billion in 2019, according to statistics published in the health policy journal *Health Affairs*. That total is expected to rise to more than $186 billion in 2027—that's nearly the same amount expected to be spent on dental services across all age groups in the United States.[3]

Other areas of senior care are also booming:

The Durable Medical Equipment, or DME, industry, is mostly covered by Medicare and is expected to be a $70 billion industry by 2025.[4]

The Senior Housing Market, which includes independent living, assisted living, memory care, and nursing care, is estimated to be a $250 to $270 billion industry.[5]

All told, elder care services generate more than $400 billion annually, and their size and revenue are only going to rise in the coming years.

"Gray tsunami"

A number of trends are contributing to the upcoming spike in elder care needs.

The biggest factor involves baby boomers, the generation born between 1946 and 1964, who all will be older than age 65 by 2030, with some into their 80s. Baby boomers—who numbered about 73 million in 2020[6]—have influenced the country as they've advanced through every stage in the aging process, and they haven't even gotten to the point where they consistently need home care.

Most of the people who will contact your agency will be baby boomers in the process of caring for their parents—members of the

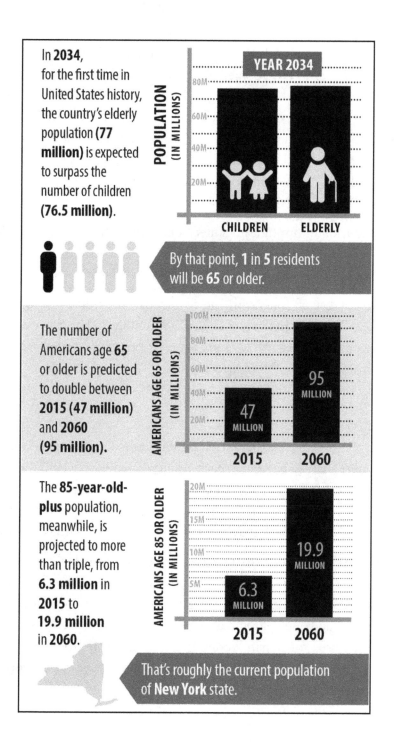

In **2034**, for the first time in United States history, the country's elderly population **(77 million)** is expected to surpass the number of children **(76.5 million)**.

YEAR 2034

POPULATION (IN MILLIONS)

CHILDREN   ELDERLY

By that point, **1** in **5** residents will be **65** or older.

The number of Americans age **65** or older is predicted to double between **2015 (47 million)** and **2060 (95 million).**

AMERICANS AGE 65 OR OLDER (IN MILLIONS)

47 MILLION   95 MILLION

2015   2060

The **85-year-old-plus** population, meanwhile, is projected to more than triple, from **6.3 million** in **2015** to **19.9 million** in **2060**.

AMERICANS AGE 85 OR OLDER (IN MILLIONS)

6.3 MILLION   19.9 MILLION

2015   2060

That's roughly the current population of **New York** state.

9

Silent Generation and the Greatest Generation—who are in their 80s and 90s. The baby boomers are caring for both younger and older relatives. But soon enough they will start needing care themselves. Medical issues will crop up, presenting physical and mental obstacles, and their children won't live nearby or won't be able to provide adequate care. And once that happens—a demographic shift that's been called a "gray tsunami"—the home care industry is going to expand like never before.

In 2034, for the first time in United States history, the country's elderly population (77 million) is expected to surpass the number of children (76.5 million). By that point, 1 in 5 residents will be 65 or older.[7]

The number of Americans age 65 or older is predicted to double between 2015 (47 million) and 2060 (95 million). The 85-year-old-plus population, meanwhile, is projected to more than triple, from 6.3 million in 2015 to 19.9 million in 2060.[8] That's roughly the current population of New York State.

Worldview on senior care

Japan and Italy have experienced similar surges in senior care needs, with more than 20 percent of each country's population being age 65 or older, according to data from the Population Reference Bureau. These countries' approaches to senior care provide examples that the United States can study and model during the coming decades.

Hundreds of tech firms in Japan are developing technology to streamline care for seniors, including devices such as ultrasonic bladder sensors,[9] which can alert caregivers to clients' need to use the bathroom, and augmented reality games for stroke patients. Robots are being used for nursing room care[10]—and despite the high cost, the technology has the potential to supplement human care efforts across the globe.

In Italy, elder care often is left to relatives, but the increasing number of seniors has fueled demand for home care services. Services are publicly funded, but the distribution of those services varies by region.[11]

Trends in aging

Our country's graying population is living longer—in large part due to medical advances—but elders are often living longer with multiple chronic conditions such as heart disease, diabetes, dementia, high blood pressure, lung disease, and glaucoma. They also prefer to "age in place" instead of moving to an assisted living or nursing care facility.

The average life expectancy for a 65-year-old in 1950 was 78.9 years. That number has increased steadily. In 1970, it was 80.2 years; in 1980, 81.4. By 2000, it was 82.6, and by 2010, 84.1. The average senior now is living to their mid-80s, making it increasingly likely that they'll require additional help for their daily needs.

People in their 80s and 90s often take multiple prescription medications daily to help with blood pressure and cholesterol and other ailments such as elevated blood sugar and diabetes.

Most seniors today, even if they require care, want to remain in their homes. That's a big shift from 20 or 30 years ago, when seniors regularly moved to nursing homes. A 2012 AARP study showed that about 90 percent of seniors wished to "age in place."[12]

A troubling trend

There currently aren't enough caregivers to cover the demand fueled by the growing aging population. As need increases—with 10,000 new seniors each day—the number of caregivers hasn't kept pace, leading to a caregiver shortage.

There simply aren't enough caregivers, and your competition is trying to hire from the same pool of caregivers that your agency is—while that pool is getting smaller and smaller. That in turn puts pressure on your agency to have enough caregivers available to provide the care you need for your clients. It's a significant challenge, but agencies can remedy the situation by prioritizing recruiting and hiring and by providing incentives in order to retain existing caregivers.

A 2019 report from the Paraprofessional Healthcare Institute suggested that the caregiver shortage could lead to 7.8 million unfilled jobs by 2026 —a mix of new positions due to rising demand and workers leaving the field or workforce.

The shortage partially is due to increased regulation. It's now harder to become a caregiver in some states because of stronger screening and training procedures.

Some leave the industry to pursue employment opportunities elsewhere.

Turnover in the home care industry is common—being a caregiver is not an easy job. Pay also is a common concern. Caregivers work inconsistent hours and on average make about $16,200 annually, with a median hourly wage of $11.52.

Caregiver gaps can make it difficult for agencies to bring in new clients. About 95 percent of respondents in the 2019 State of Home Healthcare Staffing Survey stated that staffing challenges were "somewhat impactful" or "very impactful" to their agency's growth.[13] The shortage in workers means that the costs of receiving home care are increasing.

Family care
Family members often serve as caregivers for their elderly relatives. The number of unpaid family caregivers in the United States is esti-

mated to be higher than 30 million, and those caregivers provide an average of more than 24 hours of care a week. At $15 an hour, the value of their unpaid work is estimated at $650 billion—and such responsibilities can come with a heavy emotional toll if the elderly relative suffers from cognitive or physical issues.

Many people who seek out professional home care services may have been providing care for their elderly relatives but got to the point where they couldn't do it anymore. The demands were too great and their lives too busy. With kids to care for and a job, they are a "sandwich generation" wedged between older and younger relatives needing their help.

Changes in family dynamics also have contributed to home care's growth.

Children often live hundreds of miles away from their elderly parents,[14] meaning that they aren't capable of caring for them on a consistent daily basis—giving the parents opportunity to establish unhealthy patterns like eating spoiled food, taking the wrong medication, or failing to shower because they struggle to get into and out of the shower stall.

A generation ago, seniors were more frequently living in long-term care facilities such as nursing homes, but that's often not the case anymore.

A look back

Senior care methods in the United States (thankfully) have evolved during the past century.

If seniors in the 1800s or early 1900s had no relatives they could live with, they often wound up in almshouses or poorhouses—government-run facilities for the needy. Others resided in mental institutions or old age homes.

The almshouses were for the poorest of the poor, people who couldn't fend for themselves or afford any other alternatives. They were looked down on and cast aside, society's refuse. The facilities were overrun with rats and vermin and residents bathed in dirty water.

The Social Security Act, passed in 1935, provided the Old Age Assistance program, fueling the rise in private nursing homes.

A decade later, an amendment to the 1946 Hill-Burton Act presented new opportunities to build skilled nursing facilities for the elderly. The passage of Medicare and Medicaid followed in 1965, providing seniors with affordable care options.

The number of nursing home residents increased significantly between the mid-1960s and 1980, from about 500,000 to 1.2 million. That number increased to nearly 1.6 million by 1990.

Nonmedical home care is a relatively new industry. It started gaining popularity in its current form in the 1980s and 1990s, as a supplement to care provided by relatives and medical professionals.

Home care essentials

Home care involves caregivers who provide nonmedical assistance, helping clients with Activities of Daily Living (ADLs) and Instrumental Activities of Daily Living (IADLs). ADLs include eating, bathing, dressing, toileting, and mobility.

Any human being needs to have control over those five ADLs to be able to function independently. If you functionally are not able to perform any one of those ADLs, you may need care.

IADLs are secondary activities, such as cleaning and housekeeping, doing laundry, cooking, taking medication, and managing money. The home care business is centered on supporting one or more ADLs and some IADLs.

States have different requirements and regulations for caregivers. As an example, in most states, medication management actually is a medication reminder service; as a nonmedical home care provider, you can't help the patient take the medication, you only can remind them to take it themselves. There are many other regulations and requirements that an agency has to follow in order to operate in compliance with state regulations.

Distinctions in home-based care

Despite the similarities in name, there are significant distinctions between home care and home health care—even beyond the differences in the care provided.

Home health care is covered primarily by Medicare services, while home care is not; it's mostly paid out of pocket or by long-term-care insurance policies.

Home care is also confused with hospice care, which involves palliative care for patients facing the end of their life. (Home care in many cases is a companion service to hospice.) Many home care clients live for years after beginning home care services.

Seniors living outside their homes have numerous housing and care options, including:

- Assisted-Living Facilities (ALFs): for seniors who need assistance with some daily activities but don't require nursing home health care

- Board and Care Homes (BCHs): smaller facilities that offer comparable care to ALFs but in a residential home setting

- Continuing Care Retirement Communities (CCRCs): long-term care options with a wide range of resources for those who want to stay in the same place throughout the aging process

- Skilled Nursing Facilities (SNFs): accommodations that provide full-time monitoring and medical care; commonly known as nursing homes

- Long-Term Acute Care hospitals (LTACs): specialized hospitals that treat patients requiring extended or intensive care due to chronic illness or unique needs

An affordable supplement to the continuum of care

Home care is an attractive option because it allows seniors to live in a familiar and comforting environment where everything is a reminder of their lives' memories and experiences.

Moving to a new environment can create additional challenges for seniors, especially for those suffering from diseases such as Alzheimer's and other forms of dementia. It's hard for them to navigate and determine where they are. With a familiar environment, they know the exact location of, say, the bathroom and fridge. They're familiar with the pictures on the walls. The setting still is vivid in their mind.

About 12 million Americans receive in-home services each year.[15] Home care includes anything from companionship and meal preparation to running errands, monitoring clients' daily health, and reminding clients to take medications.

One major value proposition of home care is its ability to reduce hospital costs, which are projected to reach $1.9 *trillion* by 2027. Caregivers can help seniors move around their house safely and reduce the possibility that they'll slip and fall—a major cause of hospitalizations. They also can help with meal planning and preparation, ensuring that seniors aren't eating foods that conflict with their dietary needs. Dehydration is another issue that can lead to hospitalization if left untreated. Caregivers can recognize the onset of dehydration and take corrective action before the situation worsens.

Staying on top of a senior's health and helping them maneuver through their day can diminish the likelihood of issues such as dehydration, infection, adverse reactions to medications, and slip-and-fall injuries.

Home care services are shown to significantly reduce the likelihood of hospital readmission for seniors who've recently been released from the hospital. [16]

The median cost of home care is roughly $50,000 annually, or about $140 per day nationwide, based on an average of 44 hours of care per week—whereas the average hospital stay can cost more than $10,000 for a stay stretching four or five days.[17] Median nursing home facility costs, meanwhile, range between $90,000 and $105,000 per year nationally, but can vary significantly state by state.

While home care rates are rising, in part due to compliance mandates and a tight labor market,[18] home care remains an affordable supplement to other care options.

Home care covers "a critical gap . . . between hospital stays, nursing home care, and care provided by family members and loved ones," according to the Home Care Association of America.[19] Home care operates in tandem with other care options, a critical component in the continuum of care for the elderly. It also represents a more-affordable alternative to assisted living and nursing home facilities, as well as helping families avoid preventable accidents or conditions that can lead to traumatic, destabilizing hospitalizations.

Diseases of aging

A key focus for home care involves seniors suffering from diseases of aging such as Alzheimer's, Parkinson's, and stroke, which become more prevalent as we age.

While no specific designations are required to provide care involving diseases of aging, your agency will need to focus on such care and ensure that caregivers are trained for cases that can come with specific challenges.

Alzheimer's and dementia

The most common type of dementia is Alzheimer's, a brain disease associated with memory loss and language problems. As it advances, it can make basic bodily functions like swallowing and walking difficult.

Alzheimer's accounts for 60 percent to 70 percent of all dementia cases. Vascular dementia, which can be caused by stroke or reduced blood flow to the brain, comprises up to 10 percent of dementia cases.

Most forms of dementia, such as Alzheimer's, are associated with people over the age of 60, but Lewy body dementia can strike people far younger—it's the form of dementia with which comedian Robin Williams was diagnosed before his death.

Many people diagnosed with one form of dementia could be facing multiple types, a circumstance called mixed dementia.

Symptoms

Alzheimer's disease can begin to manifest through forgetfulness and memory problems: a dropped detail, a moment of confusion, a question about something that recently happened. Signs and symptoms of Alzheimer's could include memory loss, challenges in planning or solving problems, difficulty completing familiar tasks, confusion with time or place, trouble understanding visual images and spatial relationships, problems with words, misplacing things, decreased or poor judgment, withdrawal from work or social activities, and changes in mood and personality.

The cause involves changes in the brain that can proliferate for a decade or more before Alzheimer's symptoms emerge. "Abnormal deposits of proteins form amyloid plaques and tau tangles throughout the brain. Once-healthy neurons stop functioning, lose connections with other neurons, and die," the National Institute of Aging reports.[20] The damage first impacts the hippocampus and entorhinal cortex, where memories are formed, and later affects other parts of the brain.

Stages of Alzheimer's

Mild

The early symptoms of Alzheimer's are unique to each person. According to the National Institutes of Health (NIH), they often involve a decline in non-memory aspects of cognition, such as:

- word finding

- vision/spatial issues

- impaired reasoning or judgment

Mild Alzheimer's symptoms can involve issues ranging from difficulty finding the way home to trouble paying bills and behavioral issues.

Moderate

As the disease advances in the brain, it impacts the ability to reason, have clear thought, and control language.

At this stage, memory loss and confusion can worsen, and hallucinations and delusions are possible.

Severe

Severe Alzheimer's disease sees the brain tissue shrinking as amyloid plaques and tau tangles cluster throughout the brain. People are robbed of the ability to communicate and are left completely dependent.

Caring for someone with Alzheimer's

We had a client who would not remember from day to day that he had a caregiver. The caregiver would visit his house every morning, and the first thing he would do was kick the caregiver out of the house.

This happened day after day after day. It would take about half an hour for the client to start feeling at ease with the caregiver around him and accept this person, and by the end of the day he would be fine.

And the next day, we'd have to go through the whole process again.

Alzheimer's manifests differently for each person, and that's how it manifested for this man.

It was difficult for the caregivers assigned to him—they took his rejection personally. But after a few changes of caregivers, we recognized the pattern: When you'd first arrive, he'd get angry because he didn't remember you. You had to leave the house. After 30 minutes, you'd come back, and then he'd talk to you and let you in. After an hour, you could start talking to him and helping him with his meals, and by 5 p.m., everything would be fine. Once caregivers understood the process and they could prepare for it and rely on their training for clients with Alzheimer's disease, it became a smoother process. Still, caring for those with Alzheimer's can be very demanding.

Trends

Nearly 6 million Americans were living with Alzheimer's in 2019, according to the Alzheimer's Association:

- 0.9 million (16%) aged 65–74

- 2.6 million (45%) aged 75–84

- 2.1 million (36%) age 85+

By 2050, the country's prevalence of Alzheimer's is predicted to more than double to 13.8 million—7 million of whom will be age 85 or older. That's more than the current population of the state of Illinois.

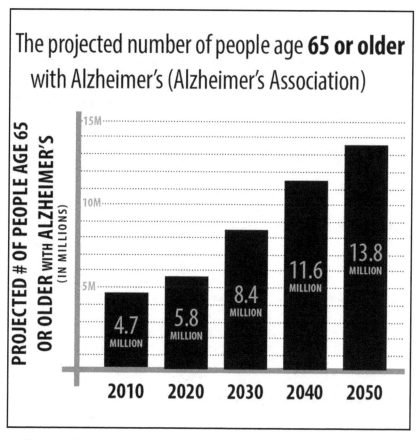

There will be more people age 85 or older with Alzheimer's in 2050 than all U.S. residents with Alzheimer's at any age in 2019.

The projected number of people age 65 or older with Alzheimer's, according to the Alzheimer's Association:[21]

- 2010: 4.7 million

- 2020: 5.8 million

- 2030: 8.4 million

- 2040: 11.6 million

- 2050: 13.8 million

Parkinson's disease

Parkinson's disease, a progressive nervous system disorder, affects a person's movement—from tremors to stiffness and slowing of muscle movement. The dysfunction of the motor system involves brain cells that become damaged and die. Whereas Alzheimer's generally first involves the section of the brain that deals with memory, Parkinson's centers on the area that produces the chemical dopamine, which is used to produce purposeful movement.[22] Parkinson's usually affects people in their 70s and older.

Symptoms

According to the National Institute of Neurological Disorders and Stroke, there are four primary symptoms of Parkinson's disease:

- tremor: shaking that has a characteristic rhythmic back-and-forth motion

- rigidity: muscle stiffness or a resistance to movement, where muscles remain constantly tense and contracted

- bradykinesia: slowing of spontaneous and automatic movement that can make it difficult to perform simple tasks or rapidly perform routine movements

- postural instability: impaired balance and changes in posture that can increase the risk of falls

A number of other symptoms also may be present in people suffering with Parkinson's, including difficulty swallowing and chewing.

Stages

Parkinson's is defined by stages, ranging from stage one (mild symptoms) to stage five (advanced and debilitating). Some people with Parkinson's can use medication to slow its advance, while with others, the disease progresses quickly. Here are the key symptoms at each stage, as identified by the Parkinson's Foundation:[23]

Stage one

- Symptoms are mild—daily activities generally aren't impacted.

- Tremor and other symptoms occur on one side of the body.

Stage two

- Symptoms begin to intensify and impact both sides of the body.

- Walking and posture problems can begin to emerge.

- Daily tasks become more difficult.

Stage three

- Loss of balance and slowness of movements.

- Falls are more common.

- Activities such as dressing and eating become impaired.

Stage four

- Symptoms are severe and limiting.

- A walker may be required for movement.

- Help is needed with ADLs.

Stage five

- Stiffness in the legs could make it impossible to stand or walk.

- A wheelchair is required, or the person is bedridden.

- Hallucinations and delusions are possible.

Caring for someone with Parkinson's

The symptoms of Parkinson's can be different from one stage to the next, so caregivers need to have training and awareness to be able to provide the best level of care and recognize if symptoms are worsening. Someone with Parkinson's generally will struggle with physical symptoms like keeping their balance and staying steady in terms of walking and holding onto things. In some cases, the person might drag their feet and try to walk constantly on their toes, giving them a higher risk of falling. If you have a client with Parkinson's, your caregivers have to be very aware of the stages and symptoms.

Caring for someone with Parkinson's involves different needs than other forms of dementia. The risk of falling is substantial, and the person may have many other challenges that require you to be cautious and vigilant.

Trends

Nearly one million people were living with Parkinson's disease in the United States in 2020, according to the Parkinson's Foundation, and 1.2 million are projected to be suffering from the disease by 2030.[24]

Stroke

Stroke is associated with disability and cognitive impairment. It involves the brain being deprived of blood or oxygen when a blood vessel bursts or is blocked by a clot.

Someone in the United States has a stroke every 40 seconds, according to the Centers for Disease Control and Prevention (CDC), and stroke kills about 140,000 Americans every year.[25] The risk of stroke increases with age—more than two-thirds of people hospitalized for stroke are 65 or older.[26]

Symptoms

The symptoms of stroke often involve:

- Face drooping—If a person's smile is uneven or lopsided or if one side of their face droops or is numb, it could be a sign that they're experiencing a stroke.

- Arm weakness—The person may struggle to raise both their arms because one arm is weak or numb.

- Speech difficulty—The person's speech could be slurred, or they might be having difficulty speaking or are hard to understand.

Other symptoms associated with strokes include sudden numbness or confusion, blurry vision in one or both eyes, difficulty walking and loss of balance, or a severe headache with no known cause. If symptoms are present, and even if they go away, you should get the individual to a hospital immediately. The faster a stroke is recognized and confirmed, the faster recovery can begin.

Types of stroke

There are a number of different types of stroke:[27]

- ischemic: a stroke caused by a clot obstructing the flow of blood to the brain

- hemorrhagic: a blood vessel rupturing and preventing blood flow to the brain

- Mini-strokes, or transient ischemic attacks, also can occur due to temporary blood clots. The severity of the stroke depends on the location in the brain where the stroke occurs, but it can lead to impaired cognition, memory, movement, speech, eating and swallowing, and self-care.[28]

Caring for someone with stroke

Proper care for stroke victims is both proactive and reactive.

It's imperative to develop a care plan around the person's unique needs after they suffer a stroke. Some side effects from a stroke can diminish and go away over time; others will not. Patients may have weakness in a limb that requires them to walk with a cane in the weeks and months after a stroke, but they may not need the cane once their strength returns.

Other types of stroke can cause someone to be unable to swallow solid food. In that case, food must be puréed and/or combined with a thickening agent. Also, the amount of food put into every bite has to be small and the texture creamy and smooth.

Lifestyle changes can lower the risk of another stroke, but one in four stroke survivors will suffer another.[29] It's vital for caregivers to recognize the symptoms of a stroke and to seek help for clients immediately if any symptoms arise.

Trends

While it's difficult to predict the likelihood of strokes, experts believe that the number of Americans experiencing strokes will more than double between 2010 and 2050—with much of the increase occurring for those 75 or older.[30] The rising occurrence of strokes expected in the coming decades will have a deep impact and require significant attention from the senior care and medical industries.

Diabetes

Diabetes occurs when someone's blood sugar is too high; their body struggles to process food for energy. Normally, a hormone called insulin helps glucose, or sugar, reach cells for energy. But with diabetes, the body's production of insulin is insufficient, and glucose builds up in the blood stream and fails to reach the cells.

Diabetes increases the likelihood of complications such as strokes and heart attacks, as well as falls and fractures, functional decline, and muscle loss.[31]

Symptoms

Diabetes can come with a wide range of symptoms, and those symptoms are often so mild, at least initially, that people who have diabetes might not even notice. According to the National Institute of Diabetes and Digestive and Kidney Diseases, symptoms include:[32]

- increased thirst and urination
- fatigue
- blurred vision
- unexplained weight loss
- tingling or numbness in the hands or feet
- increased hunger

Types of diabetes

There are two main types of diabetes:

type 1:

Normally diagnosed in childhood or young adulthood, Type 1 diabetes occurs when the body fails to make insulin, requiring people with this type of diabetes to take insulin daily.

type 2:

Type 2 diabetes can be diagnosed at any age, but mainly impacts middle-aged and older people. This type of diabetes signifies that the body is not making or properly using insulin, and it can be caused by lifestyle or hereditary factors.

Some women can develop gestational diabetes while pregnant. Other forms of diabetes can be inherited or related to cystic fibrosis.[33]

Caring for someone with diabetes

Managing blood sugar—or glucose—levels is important for those with diabetes, and so is managing blood pressure and cholesterol.[34] Establishing healthy habits can ensure that symptoms remain mild. A caregiver can help someone with diabetes prepare healthy, low-sodium meals and can also encourage them to engage in physical activity to ensure that they remain as active as possible. Additionally, a caregiver can monitor the person's medication schedule to ensure that they stay on track.

Trends

More than 30 million Americans—9.4 percent of the population—had diabetes in 2015. That rate is projected to increase to one-third of the population[35] by 2050, in large part because of the rising aging population.

Accidents and falls

Falls are a significant concern for seniors. Every 11 seconds, an older adult receives emergency room treatment for a fall, according to the National Council on Aging. Prevention of falls is crucial, and every precaution should be taken to make a senior's living space safe for them to navigate. That could mean railings installed in the bathroom, walkers used in specific parts of the home, or particular rooms or tasks avoided without a caregiver's or a relative's help.

Causes

Falls are attributed to a number of causes:

- worsening reflexes, eyesight, and hearing
- health conditions that impact balance, gait, or muscle strength
- foot pain and improper shoes
- medications that can cause confusion and dizziness

Caring for someone who's fallen

If a client has fallen, 911 should be called immediately, along with the client's family.

An internal review should focus on what happened, whether the caregiver played any role in the fall, and which mechanisms should be in place to prevent a similar situation from occurring. The assessment should highlight any and every change in the senior's life: Did a prescription change? Did they get new glasses?

Trends

Falls are blamed for 800,000 hospitalizations and more than 27,000 deaths each year in the United States, and one in four Americans age 65 or older falls each year. The incidence of senior fall-related injuries is going to spike in the coming decades as the elderly population increases, presenting renewed need and opportunity for home care services.

The most important thing

Care is a word that gets used a lot in the industry. It's in the name of the service, and the workers who provide the service are known as caregivers. But the word *care* has a deeper meaning. Care means concern or empathy for clients, that you genuinely regard and consider their well being and that you ensure that your agency is doing everything possible to improve their lives.

Care also means paying attention to detail, keeping close watch on any changes in a client's condition, and ensuring that everything done by your agency is carried out with professionalism.

Care is your agency's central focus: care for your clients and employees, care about your agency's efforts, and care in the services provided.

That care extends to your decisions for starting your home care agency too—decisions that will shape your agency's path and guide your journey forward.

CHAPTER 3

Choosing a Business Model That Works for You

Now it's decision time.

The home care agency you pursue could involve three different models: You could launch an independent agency, start a franchise, or buy a company that's already up and running. Each option comes with its own benefits and obstacles.

Let's go through each model and consider the potential rewards, as well as the challenges you'd face.

Independent Agency

Running an independent agency is the least expensive to start, but will take the most work to get the agency off the ground. You're starting from scratch—meaning there's no built-in network of caregivers and clients, no proven company structure, and no established resources.

That means it will be up to you to do the heavy lifting to get the company up and running. That won't be easy! The process could take a year or more.

Jump-starting your journey will require lots of research. It's also smart to join a membership organization that can give you guidance as well as guidelines. That's one step that I took when I started my company. I joined the Companion Connection Senior Care (CCSC) network, which has been around for more than 30 years.

Joining a network like CCSC will provide you with resources and knowledge about running your business while allowing you to remain independent—think the guidance of a franchise while maintaining autonomy. They supply you with all the necessary marketing ideas and forms and templates for your marketing materials and insight on how to start hiring. They also supply you with information about the hiring and training processes.

It might cost $15,000 to $25,000 to join a network, but you'll get access to other network members and lots of resources. And unlike a franchise, you won't have to pay ongoing royalty fees.

Those connections and resources are crucial. I learned many lessons by being able to chat with other agency owners about issues and problems and get their feedback. The insights I gained were so valuable as I started my company, helping me avoid lots of trial and error on my own.

Franchise

Becoming a franchisee means you're joining an established network with a recognized name.

You have access to resources that you wouldn't with an independent agency. Some of the guesswork is gone. There's a lot less heavy lifting too.

However, the resources, network connections, and brand recognition come at a cost. Getting into a franchise requires an initial investment of anywhere from $35,000 to $300,000.

Annual franchise fees or royalties will cost more based on the number of seniors in a particular area and the potential for that market.

Here's how the top 10 home care franchises compare in the range of initial investments:

- Comfort Keepers: 650 locations, $91,161–$144,964

- Home Instead: 600 locations, $110,000–$125,000

- Visiting Angels: 560 locations, $83,008–$128,885

- Interim: 550 locations, $125,500–$198,500

- Right At Home: 465 locations, $80,150–$147,150

- Synergy: 316 locations, $38,000–$160,000

- Home Helpers: 315 locations, $84,750–136,900

- BrightStar: 310 locations, $93,048–$154,307

- Senior Helpers: 285 locations, $105,300–$144,300

- ComForCare: 200 locations, $96,150–$286,650

There are positives and negatives of joining a franchise.

Once you become a franchisee, they train you in their methods. They teach you their methodology and how they do things. The branding and other important marketing decisions have already been made. In addition, there is continual ongoing support for marketing, promotion, and training as the industry changes. And that's why you pay them the royalty fee on an ongoing basis.

The ongoing royalty fee you pay as a franchisee is based on your gross revenue. Those payments can really add up and cut into your net profit. For example, if you have an annual revenue of $1 million and your royalty fee is 6 percent of your gross revenue, that comes out to $60,000. Let's assume your net profit is 16 percent, or $160,000. So, more than a third of your net profit—37.5 percent—will wind up going toward your franchise fee.

I know a lot of very successful franchise operations. A franchise works for some people, and there are some solid advantages—the biggest one is reducing the risk of going out of business.

If you're a franchisee, because of the training and know-how and all the knowledge provided to you, your chances of success are higher, and you can get your company running more quickly in the right direction. There's less guesswork and sweat equity needed with a franchise. But you're also more limited in what you can do as an operator. It's not as easy to make changes, develop new services, or implement innovative ideas or methods.

Buying an existing business

A third option is buying an agency that's already up and running.

The first step is to find such an agency. There are lots of resources online that list businesses for sale, and some business brokers deal only with home care companies. It's smart to contact specialized brokers.

You also can contact companies in your community and express your interest in entering the industry.

Buying an existing agency has tremendous advantages. The company already has done the hard work, spending five or ten years taking on the heavy lifting of making the business successful and overcoming those early make-or-break struggles. Most businesses sell after they have matured and are able to show a track record of success, meaning they've already met the initial challenge of marketing and establishing relationships with referral sources to acquire customers and establish a network of caregivers.

One big advantage of this approach is that you'll start making money on day one, and that's not necessarily true with other models.

Another advantage: The previous owners often stay involved with the company for some time, usually for several months, and that connection can be so valuable. You can learn the details of how the business operates, where they get their customers, and how they hire their caregivers.

It takes a while to transition from an existing owner to a new one, especially if the business has been around for a long time. You don't want to jump into the business and take over without the previous owner's involvement, because you really could use their input and insight, as well as their help becoming familiar with existing clients. Getting comfortable with hiring and recruiting practices and learning the company's processes will take time.

But there are risks, too. It's extremely important to conduct a deep and thorough analysis of the company's financials—you want to verify everything. While you may trust the owner who's selling the company, you need to verify every single detail.

A profit and loss (P&L) statement will show you the company's income and expenses, and the P&Ls and the balance sheet have to be verified and confirmed with tax returns. You need to verify bank accounts and payroll numbers and make sure that the business doesn't owe huge amounts of money, that their payroll taxes have been paid, and that their accounts receivable is in a good shape. You should request financials and tax returns from at least three years back, if not longer.

Is the company facing lawsuits or litigation? Is it expecting lawsuits or litigation?

You must do due diligence and make sure the business is clean. You don't want to buy an agency and find out that there's a lawsuit pending. And you want to make sure that you're protected over the next few years if any professional problems arise. All those details would be included in the purchase agreement.

If you want to buy an existing business, make sure that your attorney, along with your bookkeeper and your accounting firm, can help you understand the company's financial details and recognize any potential red flags. It is not uncommon that sellers try to hide something, and the buyer's job is to investigate every detail.

It's important to understand why someone is selling their company. What is the agency's story? Maybe it's as simple as the owner moving or retiring or planning to enter a new field. Maybe the company has struggled in recent years. The reasons could be simple or complex, innocent or questionable, but it's important to know the truth.

Once you feel comfortable, you can negotiate a sales price. That price will be based on an evaluation, which is usually 2 to 6 times the net profit. So, if a business is bringing in $200,000 of net profit per year, the company could be valued at $400,000 to $1.2 million. The sales price also will depend on the financial shape of the company, its rate of growth, referral sources, and the business model. For example, the stronger the referral sources, the higher the multiple. Also, agencies that are growing faster can demand a higher multiple because of their year over year revenue increase.

Working with the "enemy"

In this industry, your competition is not your enemy, and they could help your business.

I know, it's a strange concept, but this is an industry where you can collaborate with your competition. You cannot look at competitors as enemies and think that you're going to crush them. It doesn't work like that.

By having friendly competitors, I was able to pick up the phone and say, "I have this client, but I don't have caregivers. Do you have a caregiver you can introduce to me?" And in some cases, they introduced a caregiver and I gave them a referral fee. In other cases, I gave them clients. I knew that they probably would reciprocate at some point, and more often than not, they did. But the process was as simple as picking up the phone and dialing their number.

Those partnerships helped us build a stronger community of home care coverage to ensure that our clients' needs were met. It also helped me tremendously on a personal level; the other owners understood the specific issues and concerns that I faced while running my agency. We helped each other, and that collaboration helped make all our agencies better.

Settling on a location

I started my agency close to where I live in California, but choosing the right location required research. It's important to know the local dynamics, business climate, and population. You wouldn't want to start a home care business in a college town, for example, where the average age of residents is probably 28 years old—you might not find many clients there. You need to know your local markets.

You also need to know your competition. And it's really easy to do that. Simply Google *home care* and the name of the city where you're planning to start your business. Look through competitors' websites and learn who they are, how big they are, what services they provide, and how much they charge. It's important to know those details so that you can stay competitive and not price yourself out of the market by charging a rate that's significantly higher than your competitors'. Price yourself too high or too low, and you'll likely lose potential clients.

The Internet offers so much information and insight. You can use Yelp to see ratings for nearby agencies and think, "I'm up against really good providers." Or it could be the opposite: You think you can do a much better job because other companies are getting bad reviews.

Regulations and reforms

There's been a push by numerous states in recent years to regulate or reform the home care industry—something that can impact operations in a number of ways.

California's regulatory changes took effect on January 1, 2016, during the time I was running my company. The new law requires home care providers to register and receive a license through the Home Care Services Bureau and caregivers to be designated as employees and not as independent contractors. Additionally, caregivers are required to undergo a thorough background check by the state and to enter a statewide registry.

Those regulations have slowed the hiring process and increased the cost of hiring and training caregivers. But at the same time, they have greatly improved the quality of care. The background checks have filtered out many caregivers with questionable histories.

Although the quality of care has improved, the hiring process has become more expensive, not just from an agency standpoint but also for customers. We've had to pass on some of the added hiring expense to our customers.

In 2014, agencies that provided 24/7 care in the San Francisco Bay Area charged close to $240 every 24 hours, which came to $7,000 a month. After 2016, due to regulations in addition to changes in overtime and sleep-hour exemptions, the cost structure changed. In 2018, agencies were charging about $660 per day for live-in services, which is about $20,000 a month.

Your caregivers do numerous things for your clients, and depending on the state, there will be certain things that they're not allowed to do. For example, in most states, medication management actually is a medication reminder service. You can't help the client put the medication or the pill in their mouth, you simply remind them to take their medication. The client has to take the medication themself, or a registered nurse gives them the medication. Each state has different regulations in terms of supporting someone's ADLs and IADLs.

A state-by-state snapshot

Many states require licensing for home care agencies, and the requirements vary. You might need to sign up for insurance and worker's compensation in order to be licensed. Other states don't require licensing or validation, meaning you could begin a home care agency without any oversight or approvals.

Each state's contact information is available in the appendix to help readers determine any licensing requirements.

Resources

The home care industry is growing so fast—there's continual change on both the national and the local levels, and it's important to stay up to date with developments. The best way to do so is to become a member of national and statewide organizations and secure access to vital resources.

There have been numerous lawsuits in the past few years as a result of changes in the Fair Labor Standards Act, known as the Home Care Final Rule, that deal with sleep exemptions and overtime pay. Those changes were affirmed in a 2015 court opinion. Some agencies are not complying with the rules and are still paying caregivers based on past standards. There are law firms that specialize and represent caregivers against agencies in lawsuits to recover wages for unpaid hours worked.

Because of the complexity of labor laws, an agency could end up owing a lot more than what the caregivers were initially due to be paid. A judgment and court fees could sink a company.

When in doubt, agency owners should connect with leading organizations to ensure that they're remaining compliant with all industry changes and trends:

The National Association for Home Care & Hospice, or NAHC (nahc.org), represents 33,000 home care and hospice organizations. The nonprofit also advocates for caregivers, therapists, aides, and nurses.

The Private Duty Home Care Association (pdhca.org) was established in 2005 with a focus on nonmedical home care.

The Home Care Association of America, or HCAOA (hcaoa. org), serves as a voice for the home care industry in Washington, D.C., and across the country. HCAOA currently represents about 3,000 companies employing more than 500,000 caregivers.

These organizations have staff members who specialize in legislation, and it's beneficial to remain in close touch with them. They offer classes and meetings and are fantastic resources. Not only is it important to connect with them, but also, I believe, it should be a top priority. I highly recommend that anybody running a home care agency—especially those just getting started—become a member.

CHAPTER 4

The Foundations of Your Business

Other aspects of your agency will require attention too. This chapter covers everything you should know about setting up your business, from graphics to office setup and insurance needs.

Type of office

The type of office you run and setting you choose send a message to your potential customers.

Some companies take a retail approach and have an operation that is public facing, located in a mall or other area with heavy foot traffic. But for a couple of reasons, I decided not to do that. For one, it's expensive to start a retail operation. The rent can be very high, especially in an area like San Francisco, and the leases are long-term. I didn't see a good return on investment. I doubted that people would walk in off the street or take a break from shopping and say, "Oh, I need home care for my parents." Many people seeking home care would like to keep the process private.

I decided to start with a very small executive-office space, a flexible, scalable model for a business like this. It doesn't have to be big—you can run a multimillion- dollar-organization out of a 400-square-foot office. Your office staff might consist of half a dozen people, and your caregivers could come in for interviews and training and paperwork and to pick up their paychecks.

I also know of some companies that operate out of someone's home, which obviously saves on overhead costs, but you may end up having employees and caregivers come to your home for orientation and meetings. If you are OK with that and can maintain a professional home setting, a home-based agency may be a good option for you.

Back-office operations

For back-office operations, we looked into a lot of different technologies. We decided to go with a company called ClearCare, which has a very good, streamlined process for handling scheduling and payroll and other tasks. ClearCare has a great user interface and relies on the latest web-based technology, and their services brought all our back-office operations onto a single platform.

A number of other companies offer software to help home care agencies manage back-office operations, including:

AxisCare: An all-in-one solution that helps agencies manage caregivers and keep track of scheduling and billing and features a GPS mobile app and caregiver chat, AxisCare was awarded *U.S. Business News*'s Technology Elite award for best nonmedical home care administration application in 2019.

MatrixCare: A cloud-based platform that aids with client and caregiver management, scheduling, and billing, MatrixCare offers a point of care for assessments and visit notes.

KanTime: An advanced scheduling system means timesheets can be replaced with the click of a button, and algorithms aid in making the right matches between clients and caregivers.

Back when I started my company, many agencies out there were still using Microsoft Excel and similar programs to schedule caregivers. That took a significant amount of time. Those efforts could be inefficient and require additional personnel. The right software solution for your agency could allow you to streamline back-office staffing and save on the overhead of two or three positions that you might otherwise need if you were handling those tasks manually.

It is important to set up an integrated back-office system so that you don't have to spend a lot of time dealing with things like scheduling or payroll issues. Those responsibilities can be so time-consuming.

Using an outside company to handle back-office operations was a timesaver for me. It allowed me to focus my energy on customers and caregivers and on developing the company's marketing strategy. Without that step, it would have been a lot more difficult for me to take my agency to new heights.

Insurance

You need a range of insurance that covers any and every possible scenario. Some states may not license your agency without proper insurance, but beyond that, insurance is so important when considering the work your agency is doing. Insurance protects you and your employees in case of the unknown.

One possible scenario could involve a caregiver who accidentally breaks costly antique china in your client's house—you want to be able to have that covered by insurance. In another possible scenario, a client could fall while a caregiver is going to the bathroom. Or a caregiver could get into an accident while driving a client to a doctor's appointment. You want to make sure that you have coverage in case anything happens to the client or caregiver whenever they're driving a vehicle as part of their home care services.

Given the type of care provided by your company's caregivers, you never know what will happen next, and you can never be too prepared for anything that does occur.

Types of insurance include:

Liability insurance is crucial for a business. You're dealing with huge liability risk when you send caregivers to people's homes. If something goes wrong—if, say, the caregiver is not paying attention and the client falls—you've got to make sure that you have the right coverage.

Workers' compensation insurance protects you in case an employee or caregiver is injured or becomes ill on the job and also provides compensation for employees hurt in workplace accidents. It is crucial that a good insurance company helps you with your workers' compensation insurance because this could be one of the most expensive line items on your P&L statement.

Property insurance can vary significantly based on the location of your agency—from some coverage under a homeowners insurance plan if your agency is located in your home to other forms of insurance such as renters, earthquake, and flood insurance. Property insurance can cover such things as fires and storms, vandalism, and theft.

Non-owned auto coverage covers your liability when your caregivers drive clients in the caregivers' personal vehicles. It's vital that your insurance covers not only your office staff but also your caregiver employees.

It's important to speak to an insurance agent to make sure that you have all the protection you need in terms of your business liability, your employees, and your clients.

State organizations such as the California Association for Health Services at Home, or CAHSAH (cahsah.org), provide many resources regarding the insurance you'll need. Proper insurance coverage will give you peace of mind as you get your agency up and running.

Licensing

Beyond home care–specific licensing, you may need to register your business.

The membership organizations or consulting firms you use should be able to help guide you and ensure that you're doing everything by the book.

You also can write your business plan through the Small Business Administration's website, sba.gov, to help you structure your company and double-check protocols and required forms.[37]

W2 vs. 1099

Are your company's workers employees or contractors?

The so-called gig economy, led by companies like Uber and Lyft and Airbnb, made up more than one-third of the U.S. workforce by 2018.[38]

Many companies have been experimenting with the idea of considering their workforce as self-employed 1099 contractors instead of employees, meaning the workers are responsible for their own taxes and benefits. That's a big difference from the W2 model, where, when you hire somebody as an employee, you pay a portion of their payroll taxes, such as social security, unemployment, state insurance, and a few other taxes the employer is responsible for.

California businesses faced the heat in January 2020 when a new state law, AB5, directed companies to treat more workers like employees (Uber and Lyft refused to comply).

Many home care companies eventually would lose in litigation if they challenged AB5 in the courts because caregivers don't qualify as 1099 contractors under the government's definition of a contractor. The Internal Revenue Service (IRS) defines an independent contractor as someone who "has the right to control or direct only the result of the work and not what will be done and how it will be done.... You are not an independent contractor if you perform services that can be controlled by an employer (what will be done and how it will be done)."[39]

An independent contractor is someone who works on their own. You don't need to tell them where to do their work, when to do it, and how to do it. But that's not the case with home care caregivers. Caregivers are told where to go, when to go, and how to do what they do. So, therefore, they really should be considered W2 employees. Classifying caregivers as 1099 contractors could very well lead to legal challenges, and some states have rules in place stipulating that caregivers need to be considered employees.

Chain reaction

Your choice of a model for your agency—either independent, franchise, or previously owned—will impact the foundations of your business. If you choose a franchise model, for example, your branding, company logo, and website will be decided for you and you won't have to make those decisions by yourself. Also under a franchise, other aspects of the business have been predetermined for you, such as back-office software and systems, marketing and advertising, and recruiting, hiring, and training practices. Like a chain reaction, that one decision will have an impact on many other situations you'll encounter.

As an independent operator, you'll be starting from scratch. It will be up to you to make every decision. That is an exciting process! But it also can be daunting to take so many steps and make so many choices on your own.

If you buy an existing company, you'll have to decide if you want to change the company's branding. Such decisions will depend on the company's previous success—if the marketing efforts have worked, you probably wouldn't want to make drastic adjustments. You also may inherit leftover marketing resources such as brochures that you'll want to use before updating the company's color scheme or logo.

Whatever you decide, make sure that the branding is consistent, powerful, and professional. The logo, color, and graphics must stand out and draw in eyeballs, as well as send a strong and positive message.

Logo

Your company's logo and the colors you use form the basis of your company's brand.

There are many easy, inexpensive ways to develop a logo that will match your company's vision and brand.

One platform, 99 Designs (99designs.com), gives you access to ideas from hundreds of designers around the world willing to show you designs and renderings for your project. You review their ideas and pick the ones you like.

Other sites, such as Upwork (upwork.com) and Fiverr (fiverr. com), also can help you find designers to bring your vision forward. The gig economy in this case can be a big help as you establish your business!

Beyond developing your logo, it's important to make sure you have a brand guideline that details how the logo will be used on business cards, letterhead, and other marketing materials and how it will appear online, because you may need different file formats for each application. Designers on the various platforms will be able to create different high-resolution file formats for printing and the web.

The same color scheme should be used for your website, business cards, and marketing materials such as brochures and flyers.

Ultimately, branding should reflect the company's character. If you don't have guidelines in place, your business's brand is going to appear to be different depending on the usage and the medium. And when consistency is lacking in your overall look, how consistent are your business operations?

Website

The functionality of your website could mean the difference between securing or losing out on a client—visitors will leave your website within a few seconds if you don't capture their attention. Your website is one of the foundations of your business, a chance to give a potential client, or the client's relatives, every reason to connect with you.

It's easy to set up a business website using web-hosting services like GoDaddy (godaddy.com), HostGator (hostgator.com), Wix (wix.com), or SquareSpace (squarespace.com). You can choose a domain name and use their website tools to design your site. Most hosting companies also provide design templates that you can use to create a great-looking site. However, the drawback of using such template platforms is that they are hard to customize and add plug-ins to in order to enhance the functionality of the site.

Another popular option is WordPress (wordpress.com), which

offers hosting and professional site designs. Some of the advantages of WordPress are that a very large developer community uses this platform and that there are hundreds of plug-ins and options you can add to your site for additional functionality.

Your website is a way for you to share your agency's story. When building the website, keep it simple!

The website needs to be clean and clear and direct for mobile as well as desktop visitors. Make sure that whatever platform you use, the site is responsive, which means it will reshape itself to fit the window of the user's device. Fast load times are crucial. Tech glitches and slow loading will drive away potential customers quicker than anything else.

The website also needs to be warm and inviting and make people want to work with you.

Additionally, it needs to be Search Engine Optimization (SEO)–friendly, meaning that the site is easy for a search engine to recognize and understand. When people search for home care agencies in your area, your website should be one of the first results. We will cover this in more detail in chapter 5.

Check for typos or other errors! Attention to detail will help you stand out and give potential customers confidence in your work.

Having a readily visible phone number and email address on your website is crucial to your agency's success too. The longer that someone needs to search the site for contact information, the more likely they are to leave without pursuing your business.

A blog can help you generate better SEO results while also providing a platform for you to share perspectives and engage with your customers. Another engaging option that could be helpful is a chat feature, which is the focus of my current company.

Captiva8

Captiva8 offers a platform allowing clients and agencies to connect more efficiently, through both an app and an online chat tool.

With the app, potential clients or their families can choose specific care needs, and the app will match those criteria with an agency's available caregivers. The online chat tool provides 24/7 human chat agents on your website who can perform the same function and answer any questions that your site visitors may have.

Many inquiries that you receive will come from the children of potential clients, whose parents are in their 80s and 90s. The elderly parents may be hospitalized or may be going home from the hospital. They may have Alzheimer's or dementia.

The children with elderly parents are generally in their 40s and 50s, and they're pretty busy. The tools and functions and features on your website, such as a chat tool, make their lives easier. The chat option provides a level of sensitivity and privacy compared with picking up the phone and calling, especially if they work in an office with co-workers listening in. It's difficult to talk out loud about your parents being incontinent or unable to shower.

The chat function was so incredibly powerful for my agency. We added $500,000 to $1 million in revenue per year, by my estimation, because of the clients we were able to secure through it.

The chat option is crucial to being able to engage with customers. We train our chat agents on how to be responsive and what type of conversation to have and what information to provide. That is absolutely crucial to capturing visitors' attention and helping them feel comfortable with your agency and converting those inquiries into clients.

Mentality

Running a home care agency is a 24/7 job. You and your staff have to be ready mentally and physically for the challenges that will come your way on a daily basis.

It requires your availability at any time. You never know when you're going to get a call. It could be 3 a.m. But beyond that, it means you must have systems in place to ensure that someone is always available to answer your agency's calls and address any questions your potential and existing customers and caregivers may have.

Any receptionist service you employ should be professional in nature, involving trained individuals responding to inquiries based on a series of provided prompts.

If your staff is responsible for answering all calls, you might set up a rotation involving different employees handling phone duties at different times.

Your agency will require help from so many different people. Your initial instinct may be to want to do everything on your own, but you simply won't be able to—there's too much to do and not enough time in a day. It can be meaningful to delegate some responsibilities, to give your employees a sense of ownership and help them develop their own leadership skills. Of course, you want to keep a close watch on everything to ensure that the work is being completed to your standards.

As you lay the groundwork for your agency, make sure that you know what you're good at—and what you're not good at. From day one, resist false confidence in your abilities. On a personal level, I know I'm not good at accounting or payroll or taxes. I made sure to outsource those responsibilities because I knew an expert would do a much better job. On the other hand, I know I'm good at marketing and graphic design, so I decided to handle those functions myself.

Understanding your strengths and weaknesses will help you decide what to handle yourself and what to outsource or delegate, and you can hire accordingly to cover the areas where you're not as skilled.

As the company grows, you'll probably have to start outsourcing even the skills you're good at. You don't want to be the obstacle to growth if your company is growing fast. At that point, instead of focusing on what you used to do a year ago, you can hire and train people to perform selected tasks.

Your agency will succeed only because of the trust you foster with your team and clients. Trust is the bond that will help your agency establish consistency and thrive.

Consider trust to be a primary goal for your communication with prospects and customers—aka marketing.

CHAPTER 5

Marketing Is Not Just a Department, It's Everything

Some may think of marketing as a department or a function in a company or as one aspect of the advertising and messaging of an organization. But I have a different view on marketing—that it encompasses all the ways a business communicates to and connects with its customers:

- your agency brochures
- the way your employees answer the phone and respond to emails
- the way your caregivers dress
- your company's logo and color scheme
- the car that your care manager uses to drive to assessments
- your company's website and load time
- the look and feel of your business cards
- promotional items
- the ability of your customers to reach you 24/7, within seconds, by phone, messaging, and chat

- your company's online reviews

- online ads

And on, and on, and on…

All these things and many more make up your company's marketing efforts.

Making every interaction count

If you think that marketing simply is the process of getting your brochures out to referral sources and having beautiful business cards, you are wrong.

Marketing pretty much touches every function of your business that your customers see, feel, or sense. A strong and comprehensive marketing approach covers all these functions, which we call customer touch-points. These touch-points are moments in which your business connects with your customers and potential customers. Every interaction matters and every moment counts. A business that can manage and make these touch-points as pleasant and as frictionless as possible can stand out from the crowd since its customers will start recognizing that business as a brand.

Defining a brand

Depending on whom you ask, you will probably get a different answer to the question "What is a brand?" Google it, and one of the first results you will see is "Why is it so hard to find a definition for a brand?" Let me try and define a brand by first saying what it is not. A brand is not your logo. A brand is not your company identity and color scheme. A brand is not your product or packaged services.

A brand is the result of how a customer or a prospect *feels* about your agency after experiencing different touch-points during their interactions with you. It is the *feeling* that they have about you and your agency. It could be a feeling of trust, a feeling of luxury, a feeling of frustration, a feeling of reliability. As a home care company, you are in the business of *trust,* and your goal for your agency is to build a brand that your prospects, your referral sources, your customers, and your employees can trust.

What not to do

I want to share a story about a horrible interaction I had a with a company (I'll reveal its name later) to demonstrate the significance of a company's brand and customer touch-points.

I needed to order parts for a stove that I'd purchased from this company three years earlier. The stovetop gas burners no longer worked, and I wanted to order new parts. I called to place my order. After a few minutes of discussing the details of the parts, the call center rep helped me with placing the order. I gave her my credit card number and billing address, and as we were about to finish, she said, "Shoot, it looks like my computer just crashed, can you please wait?"

"Yes, of course," I said.

After I was put on hold for several minutes, the rep came back on the call and told me that her computer would not start again. She asked me to call back and place the order from scratch because nothing she did was saved on her end. Both of us disappointed, we ended the call.

I called back a few minutes later.

On the second call, I was connected to a new rep, who started helping me and going over what I needed, and this time we were able to complete the order. I was happy that the parts were on their way!

But within the next few days, the situation became more complicated. I noticed that there were two sets of charges for the order on my credit card. I called customer service again, this time trying to get credit for one of the charges; evidently the first order had been processed despite the company's computer crashing.

However, the person I spoke with didn't believe my account. She insisted that since the second order had already processed, I could get store credit—after returning the parts I hadn't even received yet from the first order. It was amazing to me that she simply couldn't cancel one of the orders!

I was very frustrated.

The following week, I received one of the orders, not knowing if it was the first order or the second order, since by then I was as confused about the whole thing as the company was, and I gave the parts to my handy worker to fix the burners. I planned to ship the other order back to the company for a refund once the order arrived. A few days went by, then a week and two, and the other order never appeared, but the charges remained on my card.

I called the company yet again to try to find out what had happened. I eventually learned that the parts were shipped to an outdated, 10-year-old shipping address, which was the address in the system during my initial call when the computer crashed.

As if all that weren't frustrating enough, to make matters worse, the parts I had received didn't fix the problem and would have to be returned.

"Oh, God," I said to myself.

After many fruitless calls, some mysteriously disconnecting, I'd had enough. I called my credit card company, requesting that the charges be blocked since the company was no longer helping me. I filed an erroneous-charge claim with the credit card company, and after 60 days, I received full credit for both purchases. I sent whatever I had received from the company back to them and swore that I would never deal with them again.

Some of you may have guessed that the company I was dealing with was Sears—the Amazon of the 20th century, which pioneered catalogue ordering and sold everything from furniture and tools, appliances and dishes, tires and toys to pillows and lamps. Somehow, they'd lost their way—and with it, their purpose and brand strength, before filing for bankruptcy in 2018.

Sears made unforgivable mistakes with every touch-point in my interactions with them, and those negative experiences caused me to stop being their customer. I often compare my Sears debacle with my experiences ordering from Amazon. Every touch-point of my Amazon experience is frictionless and enjoyable. If I don't like something, I simply return it. I usually get my refund right away, before the seller even gets the merchandise back.

How a customer feels about your company after experiencing these touch-points will make or break your company's brand and success.

The goal

Your company's goal is to stand out and differentiate from as well as to outperform your competitors in every touch-point and interaction with your customers and prospects.

That's easy to say but hard to do! Let's dive a little deeper to see how you can achieve this.

The elements that go into branding your company can be sorted into three different categories: the *visual* facets of marketing, the *content* of marketing, and the *technology* components of marketing. Each one of them is vital to helping your company succeed.

Visual

Your entire visual presence

Your logo, color scheme, brochure design, company car, uniforms, business cards, and other promotional items like gift cards, pens, and note pads all send messages about your company to your potential customers, existing customers, and employees. Add up these little impressions, and the result could be something memorable if all your visual material is cohesive and complementary. On the other hand, if your visual package is inadequate and clunky, people won't remember your company and brand—or worse yet, will remember them for the wrong reasons.

Those who are part of a franchise system may not have too many choices about these elements, but independent agencies have full control over the look of their visual package. Even a franchisee may have some level of control; for example, the quality of the paper used for brochures and business cards can make a difference when potential customers handle them for the first time.

When working on visual elements of your agency, it is important to create what's called a business or corporate identity guideline. This guideline sets standards for how employees in your company use your company's visual elements, such as logo usage, font usage, and color usage. Without such a guideline, as your company grows you will have a bunch of people doing things differently and therefore confusing and diluting the visual elements of your agency. However you develop and create the visual elements for your agency, make sure that they are consistent and cohesive. Also make sure that everyone in your organization follows the guideline for their use so you don't end up with materials and visuals that send confusing and conflicting messages about your company.

Your agency's professionalism should be reflected in how your team dresses too. It's important to have a dress code to ensure that your workers are dressed for success. Some home care companies require workers to wear a uniform that includes branded scrubs or polo shirts.

Content
Your "write" approach

Content is the collection of text, graphics, images, and videos that drive your website, give meaning to your brochure, and power your SEO, your blog, your advertising, and all your other marketing and branding efforts.

Writing is the most important part of your content strategy. Your writing must have a consistent voice. If you are a good writer and writing comes easy to you, that's great—do the writing yourself. But for many people, including myself, that's not the case. Because of that, I hire writers to help me with my content. I find it very efficient to work with the same writer on different projects. If you can find a writer who can help you with your blogs and develop the copy for your marketing material, that's ideal. But this may not be an easy task!

During the years that I ran and grew my home care agency, I worked with different writers to help me with different parts of my content development. If you are looking to outsource the writing, I recommend looking to online communities and marketplaces such as Upwork (upwork.com), which feature a large pool of writers who specialize in different disciplines and who charge a range of fees. These websites have filters that you can use to narrow your search for a writer with relevant experience.

When it comes to images and videos, you want to make sure that you have appropriate usage rights to include the materials in your marketing efforts. For my agency, I initially relied on image and video sites such as Shutterstock and iStockphoto. But I really wanted to differentiate my business, so I decided to take photos of our own caregivers with actual clients. These photos turned out so much more genuine and authentic than the stock images, and we were able to use them in many different marketing efforts. If you want to go this route, make sure to obtain a photo release from any caregivers and clients whose likeness you plan to use.

SEO

Search Engine Optimization (SEO), Search Engine Marketing (SEM), and Paid Per Click (PPC) are digital marketing tactics that are pivotal to your content strategy.

Some home care agencies are getting more than 50 percent of their leads online. The up-trend for online leads only will continue, and most agencies will get more and more new customers from online referrals.

Potential customers most likely will go online to research your agency and read reviews before calling you, even if they first heard about you by word of mouth.

Let's say, for example, your agency's name is PremierHands, and a family member of an existing client just referred you to a friend who is looking for home care for her parents. This potential client probably will go online and search "PremierHands home care agency," "PremierHands reviews," "PremierHands home care reviews," or another similar phrase.

It also may be the case that by the time the potential client wants to research your agency, she's forgotten the exact name. In that case, she simply might search for home care in your city. In any case, it is essential that you understand the basics of search techniques.

Otherwise, you could lose referrals that come to you even through friends and other word-of-mouth sources.

Driving visibility

In the above example, the search results presented by Google fall into three categories. The first category that the person sees shows paid search results—businesses will pay for placement near the top of the page. The first three or four listings on the page, as well as the bottom three listings, are ads for home care providers in your area including yours if you are doing any PPC Google Ads advertising.

So, imagine that a prospect referred to you by word of mouth now sees the top three to seven competitors in your area. Hopefully you are one of them! But if you are not spending any money on Google Ads, you won't show up in those areas.

The next category that the prospect will see consists of what Google calls the Local Business Listings or the Map Pack or Local Pack (the term *Google 3-Pack* is sometimes used). This category lists several home care agencies that appear on a Google map near the area where the person is searching. Google started widely selling ads in this category in 2017. So, the first listing in the Local Business Listings section is sometimes also an ad (the listing will feature the word *Ad* in boldface).

At this point, you are perhaps asking: How do I get my agency to appear in search results for Google's Local Business Listings? The first thing you need to do is complete a Google My Business Listing profile. By doing this, you are claiming ownership of your agency and confirming that your business is a local business with a local physical address.

Google will verify your eligibility by sending you a postcard in the mail with a special code, and once verified, you are one step closer to being listed in the Map Pack search results. But the chances of getting listed are not very high if you are in a very competitive marketplace like San Francisco.

The Map Pack also displays ratings that are powered by Google Reviews. Positive reviews can help you get listed in the Map Pack and also can help with your overall SEO strategy. People are able to leave comments and rate your company on Google Reviews as well as on websites like Yelp. The reviews aren't always accurate, and in fact, sometimes positive reviews are harder to find on such sites. Review sites are a necessary reality in today's business world, for better or worse, and you'll have to monitor them consistently because they likely will serve as a resource for people interested in working with your company.

One way to be proactive about online reviews is to ask clients and caregivers to post reviews of your agency. Hopefully you will have a lot of good reviews. It's OK even if you have a few low ratings as long as your overall rating is between 4 and 5. The more reviews the better, as your chances of getting listed in the Map Pack will increase. Of course, the other way to get listed there is to pay for a Map Pack or Local Listing Google Ads campaign.

Organic search results

We've covered the top and the bottom portions of the search engine results, which constitute the advertising section, and the only way to appear there is to pay for Google Ads. Next, we highlighted the Local Business Listings, or Map Pack. To appear in this category, you have to complete your Google My Business profile and start receiving Google Reviews. Even with that, there are no guarantees your agency will appear in the Map Pack if you are in a highly competitive market.

The third and *most important* category on the search results page shows the organic search results—a reflection of your overall SEO strategy.

Google looks to promote websites in the organic search results section that feature three elements: expertise, authoritativeness, and trustworthiness (E-A-T). According to Google, "A high-quality page should have a beneficial purpose and achieve that purpose well."[40]

Content marketing

One way to drive organic search results—while establishing brand awareness and positioning yourself as an industry expert—is through content marketing.

Content marketing brings added value to your website, which gives search engines such as Google more reason to amplify your site; this in turn should cause more customers to find your site in the search results.

In essence, it's another tool to help you establish your brand. The people seeking your services, by and large, are making difficult decisions about the care their loved ones receive. They want to work with a home care provider they trust, someone they feel has their loved one's best interests in mind.

The content marketing on your website could be reflected in a blog where you address some of the questions potential customers might have:

- What is home care?

- What are the top 10 reasons for using home care?

- Why is home care becoming more widely used?

- How can home care help your loved one improve their life?

- How can you help a loved one avoid slips and falls?

- How important is proper nutrition for senior health?

Content marketing, if done effectively with proper and targeted keywords, will drive traffic to your website and showcase your firm's proficiency and professionalism. It will help people find your site, and it will make people even more impressed when they find useful content that is relevant to their search terms.

Content marketing can take so many different forms, from blogs and videos to email newsletters and marketing campaigns. It's all meant to build trust and boost your brand by driving search engine traffic to your website.

Organic search results rates as the most important tool or platform for growing your business. Google's organic search section lists only 10 businesses on the first page of results, and that's it. In a market like San Francisco, you have to compete with hundreds of agencies to be listed among the first 10.

This is sometimes very hard to do and takes a lot of effort. But it's possible. And it could pay off in substantial ways.

How do you appear in this section? If I knew the answer for sure, either I'd be working for Google or I'd have been sued by Google. No one knows the exact formula for how this works (and Google keeps changing and enhancing the formula), but many people have general ideas on how to develop strategies that could help your business show up in the organic search results. Let's review some of them.

There is an entire industry that provides services and solutions to help businesses appear in the first 10 listings of Google's organic results page. As mentioned before, the practice adopted by these firms and consultants is called Search Engine Optimization, or SEO. During my years of running my home care agency, several companies large and small sold me on the idea that they would help me with our SEO, and some of them charged me several thousand dollars a month.

In most cases, the results they provided did not translate to a good return on my investment. So, I decided to learn as much as possible about the process, and by doing so, I was able to figure out the best methods that my agency needed to do to generate results. Simply put, there are two types of SEO strategies you can adopt: One is called on-page SEO, the other, off-page SEO. The main difference is that on-page SEO refers to those factors that you can control on your website, and off-page SEO refers to those factors that are not on your site but affect its ranking.

On-page SEO

There's more to be done to ensure that your website is getting the attention it deserves.

Google crawls the content of your website—meaning that it uses software to scan for new pages and material and adds those to its index. "Useful" content has added search value, as does your website's load time and usability on mobile devices. "Relevance" basically is what your website says you do or provide. If your website has been optimized with certain keywords, it is more relevant when someone searches for those keywords in Google. Relevance does not necessarily mean that your site will be ranked higher, it only means that it is a good match for someone's search. For example, if the content of your website has been optimized for *home care and Alzheimer's care in San Francisco, CA*, then when people search for those terms, your website has a high relevance factor.

In order to optimize your on-page SEO, you should ensure that your content is unique and valuable, with a strong match between the website's keywords and the content delivered. Unique and valuable content is usable and linkable. Users read unique and relevant content, and other websites may link to that content, which elevates the authority of your site.

The second most important factor, after your content, is your HTML title tag. Google uses your HTML title tag to display your website's information in the search engine results pages (SERPs)—which is what the user sees in the organic search results as the title that appears on the first line of the search results. To edit or change this tag, you need to edit the HTML code of your site. Most content management systems like WordPress allow you to do that easily. The title tag is designated by the following code:

<head> <title> example title </title> </head>

The optimal format for your title should be between 55 and 60 characters, according to the Boston-based software and data trends company SEMrush.com.[41] It should include a primary keyword, a secondary keyword, and a company name. For example, the following is an optimal title tag for a home care agency in San Francisco:

<head> <title> home care San Francisco - Specializing in Alzheimer's | PremierHands </title> </head>

So far, we have covered the importance of on-page SEO techniques. But in order to show up on Google rankings, relevance alone does not suffice. You also will need to work on your off-page SEO strategy.

Off-page SEO

Off-page SEO refers to actions that occur outside your website which affect your ranking in search engine results pages. The most important of these actions is link building. Having high-value links to your website increases the authority of your site, therefore increasing its ranking in Google SERPs. For example, if your agency specializes in Alzheimer's care in San Francisco and the San Francisco's Alzheimer's Association chapter links from its website to one of your pages, that's a very high-value link from Google's perspective. Google knows that San Francisco's Alzheimer's Association is a high-value site and that they have thousands of visitors who read their content—therefore, if you have a link from them, you also must have valuable content. These links boost your site's reputation. You're seen as a trusted source.

Other important ways to build off-page SEO is through social media marketing, guest blogging, and news releases. These activities all create external links to your site.

Having Facebook, LinkedIn, Twitter, Instagram, and other social media accounts may not help you directly in finding clients, but they create off-page SEO signals that help boost your ranking in Google SERPs. And that's really the optimal goal: to be found on the first page of organic search results when someone looks for home care in your area.

The value of leads

By 2017, my agency appeared in three to four places on the first page of Google search results, and we got many leads.

It's great if you appear in organic search results. But it's even better when you appear more than once on the first page of results. This is like a 1-2-3 knockout punch. When you show up several times on the first page, viewers grant you more authority and most likely will consider clicking on one of the links to visit your site. One way to appear in three to four spots on the first page is to participate in

Google Ads, meaning to purchase an ad to appear as one of the top three to four listings or the bottom three listings on the page. The second place you can appear is the Google Local Business Listings, or Map Pack. To recap: You want to make sure that you claim and verify your business as a local business, and you may have to purchase Map Pack ads if you are in a super competitive area. With your on-page and off-page SEO efforts, you also will start appearing in the organic search results. With this 1-2-3 punch approach, you will knock out your competitors and position your agency for prominence and for capturing high-quality leads.

Leads have different values for every business. If your business sells picture frames, for example, a lead that converts to a client may have a value of a couple hundred dollars. However, in the home care business if a lead converts to a client, depending on where your agency is and how much you charge, a converted lead could generate $15,000 to $20,000, on average.

But what if this was a 24/7 client who stayed with your agency six months and your agency was in the San Francisco Bay Area? In California, if a caregiver stays at a client's home 24/7, the caregiver's pay includes time and half for their sleep time. Granted, in many 24/7 cases, the caregiver's sleep is interrupted, so they usually don't get a full night's sleep. With this in mind, and the fact that agencies charge $28 to $32 an hour for 24/7 cases, the hypothetical client would bring an agency about $112,000 to $138,000 in six months.

All of this in part because the agency's name popped up first in Google search results.

In our industry, leads that convert to clients have very high value. Therefore, it is worth spending time and allocating resources to lead generation. If you want to know the value of your agency's average client, go to captiva8.com and use the Client Value Calculator at the bottom of the home page.

Technology

Your website should load quickly, and all the necessary information must be straightforward and easy to find. You need to ensure that the user experience on your website is stellar. Have people test the website and search for glitches or dead links.

Think of disruptions in web service as outages to a bricks-and-mortar store. Your website must work properly and load quickly, otherwise potential clients will depart—right to your competitors.

After all the hard work of branding, content marketing, on-page and off-page SEO strategizing, and online advertising efforts, your company's website is ready to work for you. Potential customers now are finding you and landing on your site.

But I have to give you some bad news.

You have only *eight seconds* to capture visitors' complete attention or they are gone!

If they don't immediately find what they are looking for, such as your phone number or the services you offer or an article or blog post that addresses their concern, they will click the back button and they are gone. Yes, bye-bye!

The fact is that more than half of your website visitors will leave your site without taking any action.[42] After all the effort it took you to draw them in, the majority just leave. The main reason is that they have too many choices. If you don't engage them immediately and they feel like you can't answer their questions, they will go on to the next agency. It's as simple as that.

This is where technology plays such an important role in capturing the attention of the leads who come to your website.

First, you need to know how the visitors to your site found you. By knowing that, you can track and measure the outcome and put more resources toward your most successful efforts.

Most small businesses don't know where their online leads come from. Did they start their search on Google, Bing, or Yahoo? Did they then go to Yelp and call you? Or did they call you directly from the search engine results? Did they click on an ad, or did they click on organic results? Were they initially referred to you from a hospital, or did they simply search for a generic term like *home care*?

It's really important to know the answer to these questions, because you then can decide where to allocate more resources. If you get more calls as a result of Bing vs. Google, you want to know that, so you can put more emphasis on Bing. If you get more results or higher-quality results from organic searches vs. Google ads, you may want to boost your on-page and off-page SEO efforts. Many companies spend thousands of dollars on organic search efforts, Google ads, Yelp ads, content marketing, and even traditional face-to-face efforts without knowing exactly how their customers are finding them. But there is a solution for that. It's called call tracking.

Call tracking and DNI

Call-tracking technology works by embedding a code in your website that allows for Dynamic Number Insertion (DNI).

Here is how DNI works: You get a pool of phone numbers from the call-tracking vendor you're using to track calls coming to you via different marketing channels. You get maybe five, ten, or even 100–plus different numbers. Next, you assign each online and offline marketing channel to a specific phone number, and those different numbers then can be forwarded to your main line.

For example, let's say you send out promotional mailers to people in five different cities in your area. From the pool of numbers provided to you by the call-tracking vendor, you print a different phone number on mailers for each city. Mailers that go to city A have a different phone number than do mailers that go to city B. When people call you, you will know which cities are producing more leads and conversions because they are calling those specific phone numbers. This is a simple example of how call tracking works in an offline marketing campaign. It is a bit more involved for online campaigns.

The way that online campaigns track the source of leads to your website is with DNI technology. When a visitor searches online for home care and they end up on your site, depending on how they ended up there, a dynamic phone number is generated on the site that is specific to the source of the lead. Basically, visitors see different phone numbers depending how they were referred to your site. Visitors coming from Google organic searches, for example, will see a different number than will visitors coming from Yahoo or Bing. Similarly, visitors coming from Google Ads will see a different number than will visitors coming from Yelp.

DNI works in the background to sort everything for you so that when you look at your Key Performance Indicator (KPI) reports, you will see how many leads you got from each online source. As they say, you can't measure what you can't track. By analyzing the tracking data provided by your DNI vendor, you can determine which sources are sending you the most leads, and by knowing that, you can decide how to allocate your resources most effectively. You no longer have to rely on guesswork or a blanket approach to your marketing.

Live Chat

Another technology that can drastically boost lead capture from your site is a professionally trained human-based chat extension. Online chat solutions have been around for a number of years, but many don't provide an effective solution to converting your site visitors to leads. Specifically, those chat solutions that are based on Artificial Intelligence (AI) and robots don't work very effectively in health care–related conversations. These conversations usually are too personal and complex for AI to understand and provide answers to. Therefore, the chat vendor you pick should be handled by actual humans who know your business and can have a conversation with your site visitors 24/7.

Human expertise combined with technology is the driving force behind our new chat platform, Captiva8, which is an easy and efficient way for potential clients to connect with your agency.

An online chat tool is powerful because it ties all the elements of marketing together. It is discrete and private, since potential customers don't have to converse on the phone. It's immediate and simple, because they don't have to use their phone to dial a number and talk to someone. It presents value to the customer because it's frictionless, immediate, and easy to engage with.

You want people to have a warm, trusting feeling for every interaction with your company. Too often (such as the Sears example I gave earlier), companies lose sight of that fact. They take customer interactions for granted or fall back on the reputation their brand has acquired over the years, thinking that customers will stick with them no matter what.

By and large, that's not the case anymore. Customers want the best service possible—and they want it *now*! We live in a "now" economy. Everything these days must have immediate results. And if customers can't get those results from one place, they'll look somewhere else.

Remember the eight-second rule.

If you can engage *now* and provide solutions, you'll get the work. And if not...people will go elsewhere.

Building your brand means steady, consistent effort in all the aspects that we discussed in this chapter. Recognize what's effective and continue to do it, again and again, until you achieve a level of balance. Keep up the effort, and the agency's momentum will one day fuel itself.

Your goal is to reach sufficient momentum that your marketing efforts fuel your agency like a flywheel.

CHAPTER 6
Flywheel of Home Care

It takes so much effort to get your company operating at full speed—but once you do, it's difficult to stop the momentum.

Jim Collins highlighted this in his 2001 book *Good to Great*, which addresses why companies succeed and fail. In his book, Collins used the flywheel, a huge metal disk mounted on an axle, as his model. It's tough to get a flywheel moving! Initially, you push and push, and the flywheel might move a few inches.

But you keep pushing and pushing. You put your entire force behind it. And the flywheel eventually starts to pick up speed.

As Collins writes:

At some point—breakthrough! The momentum of the thing kicks in in your favor, hurling the flywheel forward, turn after turn … whoosh! … its own heavy weight working for you. You're pushing no harder than during the first rotation, but the flywheel goes faster and faster.[43]

There is no one big push to get the flywheel moving, simply a series of consistent actions—steady progress that contributes to something bigger.

Back and forth

I earlier identified home care as a "chicken-and-egg kind of business" because it forces you to keep bouncing back and forth between attracting and onboarding caregivers while simultaneously bringing in clients.

Clients require caregivers, and caregivers require clients. At the beginning of your journey, it's difficult to find the right balance between the two to make sure that you have ample quantities of both in order for the agency to run smoothly.

The first few months, as you try to get your flywheel moving, are tough. You'll yoyo back and forth, trying to attract the best caregivers only to see them take work with your competitors since you don't have appropriate clients for them and having great clients while lacking caregivers with skills that match their needs.

There's one thing that will help you keep attracting clients *and* caregivers—the one thing generating the energy to help your agency thrive: marketing.

Think of your company's marketing efforts (all the elements we highlighted in chapter 5) as the force fueling your success.

Advertising, a well-designed website and content strategy, strong referral sources, attractive marketing communications material, and social media campaigns all can help you attract clients. Also, you'll need to recruit to fill your caregiver roles. Both client and caregiver referrals could play a significant part in growing your agency, but referrals will happen only if your company's service and employee relations are top-notch.

Once the flywheel starts spinning, you can focus on your caregivers: getting them hired, trained, and placed with clients. You also can experiment with pricing models and different programs.

Flywheel of home care

In terms of home care, a manual pottery wheel, one that's powered by a kick of your foot, is an apt representation of what it takes to get your "flywheel" moving and find sustained success.

The pottery wheel base is heavy. The base connects to a shaft that powers the motion of the pottery wheel.

The pottery wheel will start to pick up speed as you kick the base. But it's important to kick the right way, starting slow and steady to pace yourself, and then increasing your speed as the wheel starts moving. If you kick incorrectly, with inefficient pacing, you could tire yourself out and struggle to get the wheel going at the right speed.

You want to treat your entire marketing efforts in the same manner. Start slow but steady, then pick up speed while tracking, measuring, and calibrating to make sure that you are not wasting your resources.

Preparation

Preparation is a crucial step for dealing with both pottery and home care.

With pottery, you have to cut the clay with a wire and smash, knead, and pound the clay to make sure that there are no air bubbles. You could build the most beautiful pot, and when you put it in the kiln, the air bubbles will pop, causing the pot to break.

Prepping the clay takes time. But without that preparation, your entire project could fall apart.

With your home care agency, a thorough interview process and proper training program for caregivers constitute the preparation that ensures your "clay" is ready. You've done your due diligence to make sure that you've lined up the right caregivers—a process I'll detail further in chapter 8—and that they're prepared to work with your agency.

Just as an air bubble could destroy your pottery, a poorly trained caregiver could jeopardize your entire operation. The caregiver operates on your agency's behalf, and anything they do, good or bad, will reflect on your agency.

A detailed interview process will help you dig deep and uncover any red flags in order to filter out caregivers who aren't a good fit for your agency. The interview process needs to be thorough and give you a chance to really get to know a candidate. What experience do they have? What are their motivations for working as a caregiver? How do they treat people? Did they arrive on time for the interview? Are they engaged during the interview? How would they mesh with your agency's culture?

It's necessary to ensure that the caregivers you hire are properly trained and prepared for the job at hand. Some training is state-mandated, while other forms of training could be specific for your agency, such as videos or hands-on training. You need to put your caregivers in the best position to succeed based on their background, experience, and training.

That means doing your best to match the right caregiver with a client in order to ensure a high likelihood of success. All agencies will perform client assessments. These assessments often are done in-house, but increasingly are performed over the phone. Such assessments help you understand a client's needs. You ask a series of questions to ascertain the client's needs and personal information. Do they live alone? Do they prefer a female or a male caregiver?

From those answers, you can gauge how caregivers match up: Is this caregiver experienced with clients suffering from Alzheimer's?

Do they have experience managing falls? Then you can narrow down your list of caregivers and make recommendations.

Not every match will work out! If a caregiver and client aren't a good match, you'll have to be ready with another caregiver as a replacement.

The assessment and matchmaking process is precisely what we're doing with the CAPTIVA8 app and platform. CAPTIVA8 provides the thoroughness of an in-home assessment in a matter of minutes—a streamlined, efficient way to make sure that clients are paired with the right caregiver.

Working out the air bubbles will give you the highest likelihood of success as you take the next steps.

Throwing the clay

You've prepped your clay…. Now it's time to throw it onto the pottery wheel and begin shaping it.

If you don't center the clay on your wheel, your pottery will be misshapen. Positioning the clay incorrectly will doom your final product.

Similarly, positioning your caregivers incorrectly will undermine the care they provide to your clients. You have to make sure of what the client is looking for—the conditions and requirements they have—and try to match those conditions and requirements with the experience and skills of your caregivers. And that's really what it takes.

Every client is different. Someone recovering from hip surgery who's in their 70s will have different needs than will someone who's in their 90s and living with Alzheimer's. You have to be able to match your caregivers with clients having those particular needs. And if you make a good match, not only does it help the client, but also it helps the client's family—providing high-quality care can improve their lives. And it helps your business.

As the wheel turns...

The rotations of your pottery wheel will help you shape the clay.

At the beginning, it's hard to get the wheel started because it's so heavy. You have to put a lot of effort into your kicks to get the wheel going.

When the wheel starts moving, the rotation gets smoother and smoother—you don't have to push as hard. And then once in a while, you just give it this nice little push.

Since the wheel is so heavy, it smooths out your inconsistencies as you push it along. If it didn't, the wheel's movements would be herky-jerky and uneven, and that would be reflected in the final product.

If the wheel isn't turning consistently and smoothly, you won't be able to build anything attractive. Your results will be misshapen and flawed.

The results may be functional, but you will be frustrated with the process. You'll keep putting new clay on the wheel and hoping it comes out right. One after another, your efforts will fall short of your expectations, and you'll become dissatisfied.

However, when you put the right amount of energy into the flywheel of your business, your operation will function consistently, and you'll have a model to power the flywheel.

But you have to keep the flywheel going.

Strain and pain

Pottery making can look peaceful and tranquil, but it's physically taxing.

Your wrists ache. Your back throws a temper tantrum. It's not easy lugging the clay or sitting hunched over the wheel for hours and hours.

Jump-starting your home care agency comes with a different type of toll, an emotional one. It's disheartening to see your efforts fall short.

You're going to struggle at the beginning of your process—there's no way around it. The effort needed to get your company's flywheel moving will help you recognize what works and what doesn't. It's also a personal challenge, a test of patience and resolve.

Moment of truth

My agency's first client was extremely encouraging for me, and she helped me recognize that I had made the right decision to start my home care agency. That client was so good for me emotionally!

The client called and said she was looking for home care. I visited her and told her what my story was, how we do things and how we take care of clients, how much we charge—I explained the whole process. She had met with four other very reputable home care agencies in the area, some of them having been around for 15 or 20 years. And she picked me! That gave me confidence I was doing something right.

For my company's second client, I had a tough time finding caregivers. This particular person was receiving hospice care. It was a 24/7 case.

I spent so much time and effort making the case work. The fact that it was an end-of-life situation made it especially difficult. Since I still was establishing myself, I didn't have a deep roster of caregivers with the right experience, and I had only a short period of time to find somebody with that experience.

I eventually lined up the right caregiver. We were ready to proceed, and hours later the client passed away.

I was devastated.

That was the point in my business where I wondered if it was going to work. The business was about six months in. Finding the right caregiver had taken so much effort, and this was only my second client. The case had been so difficult and so unpredictable.

At that point, I had to make a decision. Give up or move forward with the business? Am I going to fail? Am I going to get clients whose cases are too difficult to set up? I couldn't run a business like this.

Luckily, as my marketing flywheel kept spinning, I was presented with enough opportunities like my first case, which encouraged me and showed me I could do this, and I continued.

In time, I put my experience with the second client behind me and focused on moving forward and finding more clients who believed in my approach and were excited to work with my agency.

But getting past that inflection point—my moment of truth—was really, really tough.

When it all works out

The pottery wheel is turning, and the clay feels so good in your hands. You keep a sponge handy to make sure that the clay doesn't dry out and tools within reach to correct any imperfections. By the end, your pottery is balanced and pure, and it looks more beautiful every second you work on it.

You made this. You didn't give up, and now look at the results!

It's so empowering when you have a new client and you already have the perfect caregiver in mind for them, someone you trust who will carry out their duties with attentiveness and compassion.

The flywheel is spinning, faster and faster. Everything is taking shape.

Disruption to your flywheel

The challenge is to ensure that your company's flywheel doesn't slow down. You don't want your business to experience interruptions, because then you won't have enough clients. You'll have to lay people off, or you'll have caregivers who cannot be assigned to clients.

It's a setback for the business.

You're creating your piece of pottery, and all of a sudden there's an interruption. The interruption could jeopardize your efforts and leave the pottery misshapen.

You can fix it, but it takes work. You have to get the flywheel going again and figure out what went wrong.

Internal or external factors can cause your flywheel to slow. But either way, it ties back to marketing.

Maybe it's your pricing.

Maybe your advertisements aren't reaching the right audience.

Maybe Google changed its algorithm, so your agency isn't receiving the same placement in search results.

Maybe a competitor is taking away your business.

Maybe a former employee used a site like Glassdoor or Yelp to trash the company. Such attacks could be based in reality or completely fabricated, but once they're posted online, they can do lasting damage to your agency's reputation.

If you don't have enough leads converting to clients, you'll have caregivers you can't assign. And if that's the case, they will go work for a different agency because they need to get paid.

Whatever the problem, it must be identified and addressed.

The only way you can identify problems is through awareness—staying on top of everything and being diligent about your KPIs. We had a dashboard using our scheduling software, ClearCare, that helped us track our KPIs, and I would study reports on a weekly basis to ensure that we were hitting our benchmarks in key areas and that the company's flywheel was continuing without disruption.

Full circle

You help your clients, and they help you. Your agency has more revenue, which means that you can hire more caregivers. Once you have more caregivers, you can attract more clients. With a greater pool of caregivers, you can assign caregivers with the right experience to those clients. Those clients become happier. They refer your agency to friends and family—in fact, word of mouth remains a top avenue for finding new clients, according to Home Care Pulse's annual Home Care Benchmarking Study.[44] Referrals increase the company's revenue. You then can hire a human resources manager, and all of a sudden you can interview ten caregivers a week instead of five. The flywheel keeps going.

New beauty

After the pottery is complete, you gently take it off the wheel and place it in the kiln. Under the right temperature, if you've done everything correctly, the clay hardens, and you've got a beautiful piece of pottery.

You've shaped something drab and undefined into something useful and attractive.

That perspective is an important reminder of the value of home care for clients—if done correctly, it can invigorate and bring new beauty to their lives.

CHAPTER 7

Five Simple Things We Take for Granted

After I got my home care agency up and running, I got a call from a wonderful family friend I'd known since our teenage years. She was frantic.

Her mother had been in and out of the hospital emergency room numerous times and was spending most of the day in bed. Her memory was declining rapidly, and she was losing weight. She was suffering, and her condition was only getting worse.

I suggested we do an assessment immediately to see what was going on and how we could help. I went to the house with our care manager and was saddened to see this woman's situation. I remembered her being so sharp and warm, but now she looked weak and confused. I brought up some memories, not only to make her feel comfortable but also to test her memory. She was clear about what happened in the past but blurry about recent events.

I asked her to tell me her birthday and phone number . . . She couldn't answer.

Based on the hundreds of assessments I'd done and my experience with seniors in similar conditions, my approach was to look for clues to determine what could be contributing to the person's decline—a little bit of detective work outside the diagnoses provided by medical professionals. I focused on five factors we often take for granted that can contribute to a health crisis: nutrition, medications, mobility, companionship, and hygiene.

Nutrition

Diet and weight are important at any age, and increasingly so for those over 65.

Roughly half of seniors are at risk of malnutrition, meaning that they aren't receiving the proper nutrients, while more than 40 percent of adults age 60 and older are obese, according to a 2017 report by the CDC.[45] An unhealthy diet can create or intensify someone's health issues.

"Under-nutrition is associated with more deaths after age 70, and obesity is a risk factor for a variety of chronic conditions such as diabetes, hypertension, high cholesterol, heart disease, arthritis, and some cancers," the Population Reference Bureau stated in a 2015 population bulletin.[46]

Nutritional issues can get worse when seniors are no longer able to cook for themselves. Maybe they have a hard time getting around the kitchen or they can't drive to the grocery store. Or maybe they're unknowingly eating foods that conflict with their dietary restrictions, allergies, or medication.

Without the ability to cook fresh, nourishing meals, people will eat for convenience. They'll rely on ordering in or on frozen TV dinners. But convenient meals often are heavily processed and full of simple carbs and salt—ingredients that, when eaten consistently, can cause a death spiral in someone's health.

Subscription food services specifically geared toward the elderly are a convenient, healthy option. The meals are fully prepared and need only to be warmed up, and they provide nourishment for people with special dietary needs located anywhere in the continental United States.

Silver Cuisine, a meal program for seniors by the company BistroMD, is a popular choice for home care agencies. This service features a wide range of dietary options, such as heart healthy, diabetic friendly, low carb, and dairy free.

Another service, Mom's Meals, is focused on seniors recovering from illness or surgery. Meals can be puréed if needed, and they're free or inexpensive for recipients of Medicaid or Medicare.

Healthy eating at age 65 or older means consuming fewer calories than when you were younger, since your metabolism slows.[47] Seniors should focus on eating lots of fruits and vegetables (especially those that are orange and green), whole grains, low-fat dairy, and lean protein such as chicken and fish.

High-fiber, low-sodium foods like broccoli, avocados, prunes, and kidney beans are especially beneficial.

Medications

Older Americans regularly take multiple medications, from blood thinners and blood pressure drugs to cholesterol and pain pills and meds assisting with metabolism, diabetes, stomach pain, infections, and more.

Seniors account for more than one-third of all prescription medication usage. Roughly 90 percent of people age 65 or older have been prescribed one drug in the past 30 days, and more than 40 percent have been prescribed more than five drugs during that time, according to government data. The more medications you're taking, the higher your risk of dangerous drug interactions.

It's difficult to keep track of medication scheduling and dosages. And drugs can come with significant side effects.

Seniors can face additional side effects from medications because the drugs stay in their system longer. As the metabolism slows with age and the body contains less water,[48] medication can persist in the body.

Some of the more challenging types of medications for seniors include:

- non-steroidal anti-inflammatory drugs (NSAIDs): linked to high blood pressure, kidney problems, and increased risk for stroke or heart attack[49]

- anti-anxiety medications: can cause confusion and increased risk of falls

- sleeping pills: can cause increased risk of falls, memory issues, and worsening of sleep-disordered breathing[50]

A client of ours, a woman in her late 80s, started hallucinating. She told our caregiver that there were people in her bedroom who talked to her and kids who played in her living room.

We had been taking care of this particular client for a couple of years, and we understood her hallucinating to be unusual. Most of the health factors in her life were under control. She was a 24/7 case, and we knew exactly what she was eating, when she was going to bed, when she was waking up, and what activities she was engaging in daily. But we didn't know about her medications, since that was handled by her daughter.

Our care manger, who had experience running several care home facilities and was aware of certain medication conflicts and side effects, noticed that the client recently had been prescribed a medication called Lorazepam, which is used to treat anxiety and belongs to a class of drugs called benzodiazepines.

The care manager immediately informed the daughter about the side effect that her mother was experiencing and asked her to discuss them with her mother's primary care physician. We also recommended a geriatric physician, who specialized in medication conflicts in older adults. After the physicians reviewed the mother's medication profile and adjusted the dosage of Lorazepam, the hallucinations stopped and she was back to her usual self.

It's vital to keep a close eye on someone's reactions to medications, especially as their medications change, and to create systems to ensure that their medications are organized and being taken in correct doses at the proper times.

Mobility

Loss of mobility is devastating for seniors. It disconnects them from the outside world and leaves them afraid to move around in their own home.

A lumpy rug or ill-positioned table could be life altering, turning the familiar into a gauntlet of household dangers.

Seniors with limited mobility, especially those who are bedridden, are more susceptible to potentially deadly health problems like blood clots and bedsores. If folks have trouble moving to and from the bathroom, that could lead to incontinence, and with it, urinary tract infections and other issues.

As seniors have a harder time with mobility, they're also more at risk for falls—a leading cause of emergency room visits among older

Americans.[51] Three million older Americans are treated in emergency rooms each year due to fall injuries, and 800,000 patients a year are hospitalized due to falls, according to the CDC.

Reduced mobility also means less physical activity, which contributes to weight gain and myriad underlying issues.

And yet the causes of mobility loss often are overlooked. Some of the leading reasons for mobility issues with the elderly include:

Falls: Slips and falls can cause life-threatening health complications and broken bones, hindering mobility. They also can provide clues to other issues such as balance problems or a stroke.

Anxiety: Fear of suffering a fall is common for seniors, even if their individual fall risk is remote,[52] leading to decreased mobility and diminished muscle tone and balance—factors that can in fact increase the risk of falls.[53]

Cognitive conditions: Conditions such as Alzheimer's often come with mobility problems. Other types of dementia, meanwhile, can make mobility disorienting or can cause someone to become immobile as they lose the ability to stand or walk.

Osteoarthritis: A leading diagnosis for those over the age of 60,[54] the wearing down of cartilage in joints can result from hereditary or lifestyle causes, as well as from injuries.

Many seniors are bedridden or immobile due to diseases of aging or muscle weakness. But other times, reduced mobility can be a side effect of medications, leaving folks dizzy and, in turn, making walking difficult. So, it's important to get the full picture on all factors contributing to their problems.

Companionship

Social bonds play a major role in seniors' physical and emotional health.

Many seniors living alone have been widowed recently. They're learning how to survive by themselves without their spouse by their side, to continue on without their best friend.

Children often live hundreds of miles away from their elderly parents, meaning they aren't capable of providing daily care.

It's also difficult when close friends aren't able to visit any longer because of schedule, distance, or mobility issues. The connections that define someone's life can unravel, leaving them sad and lonely. Beyond the emotional burden, loneliness can impact physical health—and increase the likelihood of heart disease and cognitive decline.[55]

A study by the Drexel University School of Public Health considered the connection between neighborhood social capital—the network of relationships in a neighborhood—and mobility of older adults. The study involved analysis of interviews with nearly 14,000 adults. It revealed that the amount of social capital in a neighborhood generally paired with higher physical mobility scores.[56] Richer social interaction and trust led people to walk around more and interact with their neighbors.

Having a caregiver as a companion can bring such a positive impact to someone's life, bringing color where life has grown dull and drab.

Hygiene

Poor hygiene often goes hand in hand with some of the other factors contributing to health problems, specifically mobility and companionship.

Reduced mobility can leave seniors afraid to get into and out of the shower by themselves. Lugging clothes and operating a washing machine and dryer may be problematic due to balance issues.

Seniors may clean themselves or do laundry less frequently. They also may begin skipping regular appointments such as the dentist that help them maintain proper hygiene.

A lack of companionship can fuel depression and with it, indifference about cleaning yourself or wearing clean clothes.

Hygiene often is one of the first clues that an elderly person might need help. And if not maintained, it could lead to significant health problems such as infections and skin rashes.

It can be embarrassing to need someone's help in the bathroom. Safety measures like handrails and mats can help ensure that seniors are remaining safe while maneuvering around the bathroom.

And help lugging a senior's laundry and operating machines and arranging clean clothes can diminish the potential for a fall.

Problems in tandem

While problems involving the five factors can emerge independently, they often appear in tandem. The wrong diet or medication can leave someone immobile. A lack of companionship can worsen hygiene or mobility issues. As a home care provider, it's important to recognize any deficiencies involving the five factors and to be aware of their interconnections in order —to crack the case of a health crisis.

The first clue

During the assessment for my friend's mother, we dove deeper on those five factors. What caused her situation to spin out of control?

First, we focused on food: what she ate, how much, when, and how her meals were prepared. She said a friend cooked meals for her.

We inspected the kitchen to verify what she told us. We found a carton of milk that was weeks past its expiration date, along with the meals prepared by her friend, which also were weeks old. Eating expired food can make the healthiest person sick and bedridden.

I also noticed that her stovetop was broken and that she struggled to use the microwave, meaning she was eating old food out of the fridge, cold. She was malnourished, which contributed to her confusion, lack of energy, and depression.

We had uncovered our first clue to what was causing her condition, but our investigation continued.

To remedy the situation, we had someone come and fix the stove. Now food could be warmed up or even cooked.

Another clue

We next looked at her medications. She had a tray containing eight to ten medications on her breakfast table, but in a kitchen cabinet we found another tray, full of expired meds that she wasn't supposed to be taking.

As part of our assessment tool, we always used a medications list and management form to sort out our clients' meds with the help of a family member or a medical professional. We often found duplicates, expired pills, and medications with conflicting interactions—which could lead to confusion and hallucinations.

In this woman's case, no one really knew what medications she took and when she took them. We decided to get an updated medications list from her primary care doctor and review it against all the meds she had in the house. With the help of the woman's daughter, we threw out old meds and organized the current ones. We created a new schedule of what to take when, which we posted next to her kitchen table.

At this point, we had found two major, basic contributing factors to the woman's declining condition.

Next steps

The next contributing factor was her lack of companionship and social life. A few years earlier, her husband had passed away. Her daughters had their own busy lives and didn't live close. She was lonely.

To solve this problem, we recommended a nice, sociable caregiver to visit her starting four hours a day, not only to help her with making breakfast and lunch but also to check her medications list and to make sure she took the meds correctly.

The caregiver we assigned to her case was an amazing fit. They got along great, and the woman looked forward to seeing her caregiver every day.

Case in point

A few months after our assessment, I visited my friend's mother again. She was a completely different person. I seriously could not believe how amazingly well this person was doing. Her memory was sharp. She looked better, she was dressed well, and she had gained weight. Her emergency room visits were a thing of the past.

This was a case that has stayed with me and will continue to serve as a case in point on how sometimes the simplest explanations can help solve the most complex problems.

This kind of turnaround won't always happen. Some clients have all these elements in check and under control, but they don't see much day-to-day improvement because they suffer from diseases such as Alzheimer's, Parkinson's, and other types of dementia. All that you'll be able to do is help with their ADLs in order to cope with their conditions.

Whatever the circumstances, it always is important when you start a case to do an extremely detailed analysis and assessment of these five elements to ensure that you take every step to maintain or improve their condition.

CHAPTER 8

Caring for Caregivers

Before starting my agency, I assumed that our focus simply would be taking care of clients. I soon realized how wrong I was.

About 80 percent of our daily challenges had to do with caregivers, not clients. Their cars broke down, ran out of gas, or got repossessed. Their babysitters canceled. They got evicted from their homes. They had family problems, money problems, transportation problems, or scheduling problems.

My scheduling staff spent the bulk of their time caring for caregivers, becoming problem solvers for them as they encountered personal and professional challenges.

A difficult job

Being a caregiver isn't an easy job.

With inconsistent work hours, home care workers earned a median hourly wage of $11.52, making about $16,200 annually, according to research published in 2019 by the worker advocacy organization Paraprofessional Healthcare Institute (PHI).[57] Wages can be much higher in places such as California, especially depending on the type of case.

Caregiver wages are influenced in part by client affordability, because every dollar that agencies pay for caregivers drives up the cost of care for clients, making home care less and less affordable. Affordability for end users is the driving force behind keeping wages low. As caregiver wages increase, you start eliminating potential clients who can afford your services.

Nearly 90 percent of caregivers are women, and 37 percent are between the ages of 25 and 44. Many are immigrants. They sometimes live together with other caregivers, sharing a car and other resources.

More than half of caregivers receive public assistance, and 18 percent live in a household below the federal poverty line, according to PHI.[58]

And yet, the job comes with stress, anxiety, and incredible responsibility. Being a caregiver is emotionally taxing. It is a hard job both physically and mentally. You're dealing with someone's health related issues and caring for them while also juggling their family's needs. When you do that as a job, hour after hour and day after day, with not just one but maybe a few different people, it becomes very stressful and can exact an emotional toll.

Caregivers are caring people—that's generally why they have been attracted to this profession. Not everybody can do it.

One of the most difficult aspects of being a caregiver is the schedule. It can be inconsistent and full of last-minute adjustments. Every client's scheduling needs will be different. Sometimes you get a referral from a hospital saying that service for a client will start in just a few hours, and then the schedule changes the very next day because the person is readmitted to the hospital.

Every customer's needs are completely different. Some require long-term, 24/7 care. Those are the easiest to schedule because somebody has to be there every hour, so you just continue scheduling those shifts.

A vital role

Caregivers are the life force of your agency, the frontline workers helping your clients with their ADLs.

Caregivers perform so many different duties. They help clients transfer from one place to another: bed and bath and wheelchair and car. They aid them with bathing and bathroom functions. They cook and clean. They remind clients when to take their medications. They drive them to doctor's appointments. They provide them with companionship.

They serve as the client's advocates and protectors and representatives and communicators and translators and mediators. Coordination with the client's relatives helps provide a more seamless continuum of care.

Your agency's training and guidelines for caregivers can furnish them with a framework for success.

Support

When you spend your waking hours caring for other people, you often can forget to care for yourself.

The stress can become a little too much sometimes—especially when a caregiver loses a client after forming a deep bond with them. The grieving process is similar to that of losing a family member.

Caregivers mourn and get depressed; even though this is a job, it's not the kind of job that you can clock in and out from emotionally. The emotional weight stays with you.

Agencies need to be vigilant about ensuring that caregivers are getting the help, resources, and support they need. Two leading voices in the industry are the National Alliance for Caregiving, which has been a driving force for caregiver studies and information, and Family Caregiver Alliance, which has provided services to family caregivers for more than 40 years.

My agency's care managers spent time with caregivers who were struggling, and we also gave caregivers paid time off when they needed it. We helped them find clients who would be a good fit for them after they experienced a loss.

The daily grind

Caregivers often face challenges in their daily lives, especially in the San Francisco Bay Area, where it is expensive to live.

One of the biggest problems we dealt with at my agency involved caregivers not being able to use their car and therefore running late. We opened an account with the ridesharing company Uber in order to transport caregivers from one case to another to make sure they would be on time. On some occasions, staff members drove caregivers to and from appointments.

Whenever caregivers don't show up for a shift, you're forced to scramble.

No matter the situation, you should always have a backup plan.

It is prudent to have two or three caregivers on call in case you have a shift that needs to be filled. Caregivers who pick up last-minute shifts might receive a bonus or a gift card for gas or coffee as a perk for going above and beyond.

Last-minute challenges are difficult to staff because your on-call caregivers already might be working with another client or a different agency, which is why you always should have a number of backup options available for ongoing cases. Make notes, on paper or in your scheduling system, about caregivers who potentially can cover cases if the main caregiver isn't able to show up. That way you easily can figure out whom to contact on short notice.

Getting the facts

From time to time, a situation will occur involving a caregiver.

Sometimes a client will slip and fall. Calling 911 and making sure they're cared for is the first step, but after that comes the follow-up, in which you need to get a thorough accounting of what happened. Where was the caregiver at the time the client fell? What happened? Was the situation preventable? If it wasn't preventable, did the caregiver do everything they could to make sure that the client was safe and recovering?

Misunderstandings are especially common with clients who have Alzheimer's or dementia because of memory challenges. A client may give something to the caregiver, and family members will later see that it's missing and accuse the caregiver of stealing.

Sometimes your staff may have to look around the house to see if anything is missing only to find that the client put their wallet in a different place.

Caregivers should be trained on these sorts of issues and instructed not to take anything that belongs to the client and to report anything that's given to them as a gift. One case we encountered involved the client giving the caregiver money during the holidays. The client's daughter later found out that there was money missing from her mother's wallet, and when the daughter asked her mother about the money, she didn't know where it was. The daughter asked the caregiver about it, and the caregiver admitted to being given the money as a gift.

In another case, a client with Alzheimer's was giving our caregiver vases and personal belongings that she no longer needed. The client's daughter later found out that the items were missing —it turned out they were family heirlooms. The client confirmed that she was giving the vases and belongings away.

The daughter was very angry that the caregiver had taken the items without reporting it to the agency or the family. We ended up terminating the caregiver because she hadn't followed our company policy requiring caregivers to report when they were given something by a client. This kind of policy ensures that everyone is aware of the situation and that if any disagreement arises, there is a paper trail.

Turnover

Caregiver turnover is a problem at every firm.

Agencies find, hire, and train caregivers only to see them take on work through other agencies or leave the industry. Between 2016 and 2026, there's expected to be 7.8 million openings in direct care—a combination of caregivers, home health aides, and nursing assistants—in the home care and home health industries, according to an analysis by PHI. It breaks down like this:

- 3.6 million workers expected to leave the workforce

- 2.8 million workers expected to leave the field

- 1.4 million new positions created due to demand

To put these statistics into context, "long-term care employers will need to fill 7.8 *million* total direct care job openings from 2016 to 2026—double the population of Los Angeles," according to the PHI analysis.[59] The bulk of the job growth is expected in California, New York, and Texas.

Caregiver turnover also is a major focus of the annual Home Care Benchmarking Study, conducted by Home Care Pulse. According to the 2019 study, the median caregiver turnover rate jumped to 82 percent, an all-time high.

A survey of thousands of caregivers revealed that scheduling was their biggest problem.

"Caregivers overwhelmingly tend to want more hours, more consistent hours week-to-week, and the ability to build their schedule around other commitments like family, school, and other jobs," wrote Connor Kunz, a project manager at Home Care Pulse.[60]

Additional pay certainly can help retain caregivers, but increased caregiver pay reduces your agency's affordability by the same level.

At the same time, caregiver turnover makes it difficult to take on new clients. In fact, many agencies have to turn away potential clients because they don't have caregivers who can work with them.

An agency's cost for replacing a caregiver typically can run between $2,500 and $4,500. If you're replacing more than half your pool of caregivers, the total expense each year could top $100,000.[61]

Increasing demand

More than 25 percent of caregivers are immigrants.[62] And while America's immigrant population is expected to account for much of the country's population growth in the coming decades, it alone is not going to be enough to offset the incoming "gray tsunami" of baby boomers requiring home care.

Increased industry regulation and deeper background checks also are diminishing the potential caregiver workforce, disqualifying some applicants from becoming caregivers. While regulation has helped to improve the quality of care, it also means that it takes longer to hire, train, and onboard caregivers.

Companies like Amazon and Target have raised their minimum wage, creating additional competitive jobs and making it more difficult to recruit new caregivers (states and municipalities increasing their minimum wage has had a different potential effect: reducing an agency's bottom line).

Despite the problematic trends, there are tried-and-true methods to minimizing turnover: recruiting, rewarding, and retaining caregivers.

Recruiting

The first step in building your roster of caregivers is the most important: recruiting.

Without bringing in a steady stream of prospective caregivers, your other efforts won't mean much—and your flywheel won't operate.

If you have a shortage of caregivers, you have to recruit more. In order to increase our ability to recruit more caregivers, my agency hired a full-time hiring manager who concentrated on recruiting, with a focus on online advertising and a robust referral program. Those efforts attracted new applicants, and we got to the point where we had more applicants than positions to fill—which is fantastic because it allows you to have a steady candidate pool while also hiring higher-quality candidates.

Recruiting can come through many sources, including your agency's website and social media accounts, job fairs, job listings sites like Indeed, and advertisements with local media. Recruiting is an ongoing process that ensures you can continue to find new caregiver candidates.

Rewarding

In this industry, little perks can go a long way.

Paying caregivers a dollar an hour more than your competitors could incentivize them to stay with your agency and reduce your need to hire and train someone new to replace them.

You have to figure out ways to help caregivers. You have to encourage them and tell them that they're doing a great job. Reward them with gas cards or gift cards to Target for their efforts. A $20 gift card will help a caregiver fuel their vehicle or buy groceries for their family.

My agency had a caregiver-of-the-month program. Every month we featured a different caregiver in the newsletter that we sent to caregivers and clients, and the honoree also received a certificate. The caregivers loved that—they were so proud to be honored for their hard work.

Make sure that your affirmation and your rewards to your caregivers are specific, timely, and heartfelt. Let them know when they do a great job, and mean what you say when you reward them.

Retaining

Retaining your top caregivers allows you to establish a firm, reliable foundation and ensures a measure of stability. You've trained your caregivers to succeed and have established trust with them. You trust them with your clients and trust them representing your agency.

The most effective way to retain your caregivers is to keep them busy with clients. Many caregivers work with multiple agencies—it's a standard practice—but keep giving them steady work, and they will be less inclined to pursue other opportunities or will prioritize opportunities from your agency.

My agency developed a lucrative caregiver referral program. If caregivers referred someone and we hired them, the referring caregiver would earn money over a period of time, sometimes up to

$500; the longer the referred caregiver worked for us, the more the referring caregiver made in bonuses. It was a good program to initiate, to market, and to grow—many of our new employees came from existing caregiver referrals.

Having a solid caregiver referral program is very important because all other agencies are competing for the same caregivers. If you can have your top existing caregivers refer other caregivers they believe would be a good fit, it reflects their commitment to your agency and serves as a tried-and-true method for recruiting top-tier talent. According to data from Home Care Pulse's Home Care Benchmarking Study, turnover rates are lowest for word-of-mouth referrals and referrals by current employees—both at or below 50 percent—while median turnover rates for internet sources generally are 65 percent to 75 percent.[63]

The bottom line

Those three Rs— recruiting, rewarding, and retaining—are so important because they allow you to build a fantastic network of caregivers you know and trust. The strength of your caregiver network will allow you to take on a wider range of clients and have better odds of making good matches between caregivers and clients.

Caring for your caregivers will motivate and empower them to do their best work. Without them, your agency won't survive. And being able to take on the right balance of clients will make or break your agency's bottom line.

CHAPTER 9

New Ideas and Future Outlook

The home care industry has many challenges and opportunities ahead.

The "gray tsunami"—the wave of baby boomers reaching retirement age and increasingly needing home care during the 2020s—is fast approaching.

In order to prepare for the growing demand, agencies will need to recruit new caregivers and reduce turnover rates. The current tendency to devalue the role of caregivers must change, and outside-the-box thinking is required to drive the industry forward. Agencies also need to embrace new technology at a much faster pace. Millions of new potential customers will be looking to engage with agencies in nontraditional ways—beyond phone calls, emails, and in-person meetings. They will expect faster response times from agencies with less friction and back and forth. App, chat, and multichannel digital engagement will be necessary to communicate with future customers.

A changing view of caregivers

Caregivers represent the front lines of a client's care.

They spend hour after hour with a client. In many cases, they know a client and their care needs better than do the client's own relatives. But they're regularly overlooked in terms of a client's health care—and often looked down on by nurses and health care professionals. The topic was highlighted in a 2019 study published in the *Journal of the American Geriatrics Society*:

One barrier to the inclusion of this workforce in teams is the lack of awareness of the complex nature of the job and the potential contributions that aides can make to achieving higher quality of care and quality of life for individuals with chronic or serious illness. Aides often are referred to as "unskilled," not recognized as professional care providers, and undervalued as evidenced by their low wages and lack of adequate benefits. Doctors, hospitals, insurance companies, legislators, and federal and state policymakers typically do not think that aides can be real members of a care team. Many of the advocates for this workforce lump aides into a broad "low-wage" worker category that encompasses services workers in hospitality, domestic housekeeping, and other industries. This labeling fails to acknowledge the competencies that are required to deliver hands-on personal care and emotional support to individuals who are chronically or seriously ill.[64]

The approaching need for senior care is going to force us to take a deeper look at the formalized division between the home care and health care industries. How can we best utilize the people and resources devoted to a senior's care? One reform could involve home care workers being trained to perform some health care tasks like applying eye drops or dressing wounds.

Training opportunities could bring better pay to more-established caregivers, incentivizing them to remain in their jobs, giving them a role on interdisciplinary care teams, and reducing caregiver burnout and turnover. Teaching caregivers new skills has been shown to diminish client hospitalization rates and improve caregiver job satisfaction.[65]

"Home care aides see their clients every day for hours," Massachusetts Institute of Technology professor Paul Osterman wrote in his 2017 book *Who Will Care for Us?* "No one is in a better position to help with the challenges of chronic conditions than they are."[66]

Caregivers play a vital role in client care, but until the role comes with better opportunities for gaining respect and upward mobility, the caregiver gap will continue to widen due to burnout and turnover.

Bridging the gap

A group of U.S. politicians in September 2019 introduced to Congress the Direct Creation, Advancement, and Retention of Employment (CARE) Opportunity Act, H.R. 4397, aimed at training and employment advancement opportunities for direct-care workers.

Two of the act's aims:

- implementing models and strategies to make the field of direct care more attractive, such as training, providing career pathways, mentoring, and allowing for local and regional innovation to address workforce shortages in a high-demand field

- encouraging retention and career advancement in the growing field of direct care

Solving pressing issues in home care will take lots of resources and attention. While the home care industry often has been overlooked, the industry won't be easy to ignore in the coming years as it experiences a boom.

Men welcome too

More than 75 percent of caregivers are women, according to the Family Caregiver Alliance[67]—they're generally seen as more sensitive and caring.

But our society's gender norms are changing, and an influx of men in the home care industry could help diminish the severity of the caregiver shortage.

Millions of men serve as family caregivers, aiding relatives with their daily needs. Those duties match strongly with the responsibilities of a home care caregiver.

"We have to challenge the false gender stereotyping that this is something only women can do," Robert Espinoza, the vice president of policy at PHI, told *The New York Times* in 2019.[68] "It hurts women because their work is not sufficiently valued, but it hurts men, too, because they're missing out on what can be a really rewarding job experience."

Most requests are for female caregivers, since most clients are female. Usually female clients want to have a female caregiver, while male caregivers are requested more regularly by male clients. A female client might request a male caregiver only if the circumstances involved the client's weight and transfer needs.

Male caregivers did a great job working with my agency, and they certainly serve an important role in caregiving, even if that's in conflict with societal views of the job.

Win-win

Another potential solution to the caregiver shortage could involve people with outstanding student loan debt, a group that consists of more than 45 million people.

Those borrowers owe nearly $1.6 trillion in student loan debt, according to data released in early 2020.[69] The average amount owed in student debt is more than $30,000. Most of the borrowers are between 25 and 49 years old.

What if those 45 million borrowers had the option of reducing their student loan debt by working in the home care industry—a chance to solve two problems at once? Why couldn't a federal loan forgiveness program pair with home care?

This type of program could be a win-win-win. Loan recipients would win because for every hour they work, they would get two hours of credit toward their loan. For example, if they work 10 hours providing care through an approved home care agency—getting paid $15 an hour and earning $150 for the 10 hours—they could receive $300 credit toward their outstanding student loan. The win for home care agencies is that they will have access to potentially millions of new caregivers, and the win for the government is that it could solve two major challenges the U.S. faces: the student loan crisis and the caregiver shortage crisis.

Home care–focused student loan forgiveness programs could mirror programs currently available to teachers, specifically those working in low-income schools or educational centers. Through the federal Teacher Loan Forgiveness Program, teachers can receive up to $17,500 in loan forgiveness after five consecutive years of teaching full time. Federal Perkins Loan cancellation is possible for teachers focused on special education, math, or science, as well as for teachers working at low-income schools. The loans are forgiven over a five-year period: 30 percent over the first two years, 40 percent over the third and fourth years, and the remaining 30 percent in the fifth year.

Home care could receive an influx of much-needed workers through loan forgiveness programs, and recent college grads could get an opportunity to reduce their student loan burden while learning valuable life lessons about service, care, and aging.

The concept may sound far-fetched, but similar programs already have launched in the United States as well as across the world:

- In Norway, a fascinating program allows borrowers who provide care for someone—including "a disabled or functionally impaired person or an elderly person in the immediate family who needs constant care and attention"—to apply for an interest exemption.[70]

- The federal government in the United States has experimented with student loan forgiveness programs, including Public Service Loan Forgiveness (PSLF), which is open to people who work with government organizations, 501(c)(3) organizations, and not-for-profits that provide a qualifying public service. But acceptance into the program is narrow and requires 120 qualifying monthly payments— 10 years' worth —before you can qualify. Of the more than 40,000 applicants by February 2020, only 206 had their loans forgiven.[71] That's half of one percent of applicants. For the 39,794 applicants denied acceptance to PSLF, loan forgiveness is available through Temporary Expanded Public Service Loan Forgiveness (TEPSLF), but the process is cumbersome.

- New York State has a loan forgiveness program in which licensed social workers, including those working in home care, can receive up to $26,000 in loan forgiveness.

- Politicians in Maine have pursued a bill that would offer

student loan debt relief for nursing students. (Home care caregivers are not eligible.)

- The National Health Service Corps in 2019 launched a loan repayment program for professionals who work at an approved substance abuse disorder treatment site.[72]

Current student loan programs aren't perfect—many come with strict guidelines,[73] have specific career focuses, or are income driven—but a program that pays down student loan debt could inspire a wave of new home care employees while also providing much-needed care for aging Americans.

Innovation

New tools are transforming senior care.

Innovation is carrying the home care industry forward in numerous ways:

- cutting-edge tech developments making life safer for seniors
- original approaches to engaging clients
- emerging platforms that bridge the gap between client and agency

In-home technology

Technology has proved helpful with senior care, presenting more efficient and effective ways to ensure that clients are staying safe.

Instead of home security systems that guard against break-ins and keep dangers out, monitoring services for seniors can rely on sensor devices placed inside the home. The sensors feed data and can alert caregivers or relatives if something is amiss, such as a fall.

Wearables like shoe insoles or jewelry also can track the wearer's location and vital signs. Wearables are especially helpful for seniors suffering from Alzheimer's and other forms of dementia who may be more susceptible to going missing. Some of the devices feature alert buttons that can be pressed if the wearer is in distress, sending alerts to emergency responders.

"Sensors, which are getting ever smaller and more discreet, can help track seniors' intake of medication and water, monitor their homes, and even save them trips outside their homes by automatically reordering their favorite groceries and cleaning supplies," Nimrod Kaplan, chief technology officer and co-founder of the smart-packaging company Water.io, wrote in an essay for *Forbes*.[74]

The sensors send information through apps, allowing a client's caregiver, agency, relatives, and health professionals a chance to monitor the client's location, vital signs, and other developments.

Sensors also can track medication intake.[75] An alert is sent when pills are running low or when a senior needs to take their medication or, through a patch, when the pill reaches their stomach.

Such technologies are less a form of Big Brother and more a solution for seniors seeking to age in place—a way for seniors to manage their ADLs and IADLs in tandem with home care.

Cameras and sensors on the tech devices constantly monitor the person without showing their actual image—a skeleton is seen, so there's no invasion of privacy. A program's algorithms can scrutinize a pattern of dots and recognize where the person is, what they might be doing, and whether anything concerning has happened, such as a fall.

My agency used video cameras and sensors with several clients, and many clients had fall detection bracelets and necklaces. It was so important to us as well as to the clients' families to have peace of mind and use advanced technology to help ensure our clients' safety.

Apps

Mobile technology presents new options for seniors and their caregivers.

Blood pressure readings can be captured by your phone and sent to your doctor. Reminders pop up whenever it's time to take medication. GPS tracking and fall detection can help you monitor seniors and ensure that they're safe. Other apps allow visually impaired users to gauge their surroundings, and magnifying glass apps help those struggling to read fine print.

Wearable devices

Wearable devices represent the next frontier in senior health.

Instead of alerting emergency responders of a problem—such as with Life Alert pendants or wristbands known for the "I've fallen and I can't get up" commercials—devices such as Apple Watch can uncover troubling trends *before* symptoms are apparent.

Apple's Heartline collaboration with Johnson & Johnson aims to recognize irregular heart rhythms consistent with atrial fibrillation, which often precedes heart attacks or strokes. Apple is working to develop additional features for the Apple Watch Series 6 in late 2020, including blood oxygen detection and an improved electrocardiogram.

The Heartline study involves U.S. residents age 65 or older who have Original Medicare, a.k.a. traditional Medicare. The ultimate goal of the program is "finding new patterns in the study data that may help to identify, prevent, or treat other medical conditions beyond those that involve the heart."[76]

Tools for efficiency

Tools, apps, and gadgets can help transform home care.

With the implementation of sensors and wearable devices, your agency may not have to spend 24 hours a day with a client. You could have four or eight hours of direct in-person care, then spend the rest of the day relying on sensors and monitors and technologies that could alert you if something happens.

Art therapy

One of the programs that my agency used is MnemeTherapy (*Mneme* being pronounced "nemma"). It was developed in the early 2000s by Noell Hammer[77] and named after Mnemosyne, the Greek goddess of memory. MnemeTherapy uses everyday pleasures such as singing, movement, painting, and storytelling in a unique combination to stimulate dramatic changes in the brain. Sessions feature therapists working one-on-one with participants, guiding their brushstrokes or leading their movement as music plays.

The program isn't the only type of art therapy for Alzheimer's patients, but I was struck by how promising the benefits were for our clients. It opened a whole new world for them.

MnemeTherapy has been helpful for children with autism, and we saw wonderful results with clients diagnosed with Parkinson's and dementia and Alzheimer's. The therapy wasn't for all our clients, but some benefited quite a bit. It was amazing to see how it brought families together and created special moments between parents and their children. It became very popular—the fact that we offered this program helped us attract a number of clients. It helped clients uncover memories that they had lost and allowed them to be creative in new ways.

CAPABLE

Community Aging in Place—Advancing Better Living for Elders (CAPABLE) is a program that teaches aging-in-place seniors how to improve their safety and decrease risks like falls.

CAPABLE, which was developed by the Johns Hopkins School of Nursing, involves a team approach featuring a nurse, handy worker, and occupational therapist. Just as caregivers can benefit from training, it's meaningful for seniors to learn tactics that will help them maintain a high quality of life and avoid life-threatening risks. In a demonstration project conducted from 2012 to 2015, participants who started out struggling with about four ADLs had difficulty with only two after five months.[78] CAPABLE helped them with shopping for groceries and managing their medications, along with reducing their symptoms of depression.

According to Johns Hopkins, the program yields more than six times return on investment—about $3,000 in program costs can result in "more than $20,000 in savings in medical costs driven by reductions in both inpatient and outpatient expenditures."[79]

Agencies can partner with such programs to offer their support and expertise in caring for seniors in cases where the seniors may benefit from having a caregiver helping with their ADLs.

A changing view of customers

The next innovation in home care involves my chat and app platform, Captiva8.

Captiva8 allows potential customers to engage with agencies in real time to find out if a particular home care agency has available caregivers. Without Captiva8, it may take a company a few days of phone calls and emails to find a caregiver to match with a particular case—crucial moments when customers can have second thoughts or wind up going with a competing agency.

Captiva8 streamlines the process for clients and agencies, employing a matchmaking approach to find caregivers based on specific care needs.

While customers can use the app and chat platform to connect with agencies and reduce their anxiety about employing home care, home care agencies can use the service to convert interested parties into paying customers, a seamless process that provides agencies a new revenue stream.

Revenue will help drive your agency to new heights—a chance to get your company's flywheel moving and fuel your growth and enable you to provide the best care possible for seniors looking to remain at home while making the most of their golden years.

For more information on Captiva8, visit captiva8.com.

The road ahead

The coming years will require diligence, support, and innovation in home care. **Caring for Millions** won't be easy, and our industry can use lots of help. But home care might be the greatest opportunity for you as a career—a chance to give back to those in need and to help clients and their families make the most of their lives.

Pour your energy into this industry and follow the right steps, and you'll be rewarded in so many ways.

Appendix: A State-by-State Snapshot

Dozens of states require licensing for home care agencies, and the requirements vary. You might need to sign up for insurance and worker's compensation in order to be licensed. Other states don't require licensing or validation, meaning that you could begin a home care agency without any additional oversight or approvals.

Each state's contact information is available below so that readers can find out on their own if licensing is required. If your state is not listed below, contact your state's Department of Human Services, Department of Social Services, or Bureau of Licensing and Certifications.

Alabama
Alabama Department of Human Resources
1-334-242-1310
http://dhr.alabama.gov

Alaska
Alaska Department of Health and Social Services
1-907-465-3030
http://dhss.alaska.gov

Arizona

Arizona Department of Economic Security

1-602-542-4791

https://des.az.gov

Arkansas

Arkansas Department of Human Services

1-351-682-8635

https://humanservices.arkansas.gov

California

California Department of Social Services

1-916-455-6951 or 1-916-654-3345

http://www.cdss.ca.gov

Colorado

Colorado Department of Human Services

1-303-866-5700

https://www.colorado.gov/cdhs

Connecticut

Connecticut Department of Social Services

1-800-824-1358

https://portal.ct.gov/dss

Delaware

Delaware Department of Health and Social Services

1-302-577-4352

http://www.dhss.delaware.gov/dhss

District of Columbia

D.C. Department of Human Services

1-202-INFO-211 (1-202-463-6211)
https://dhs.dc.gov

Florida
Florida Agency for Health Care Administration
1-888-419-3456
http://www.fdhc.state.fl.us

Georgia
Georgia Department of Human Resources
1-404-651-6314
https://dhs.georgia.gov

Hawaii
Hawaii Department of Human Services
1-808-586-4997
http://humanservices.hawaii.gov

Idaho
Idaho Department of Health and Welfare
1-208-334-6558
https://healthandwelfare.idaho.gov

Illinois
Illinois Department of Human Services
1-217-557-1601
http://www.dhs.state.il.us

Indiana
Indiana Family and Social Services Administration
1-317-233-4690
http://www.in.gov/fssa

Iowa
Iowa Department of Human Services
1-515-281-3147
https://dhs.iowa.gov

Kansas
Kansas Department of Social and Rehabilitation Services
1-785-296-3271
http://www.dcf.ks.gov/Pages/default.aspx

Kentucky
Kentucky Cabinet for Health and Family Services
1-352-564-7042
http://chfs.ky.gov

Louisiana
Louisiana Department of Social Services
1-225-342-7475
http://www.dss.state.la.us

Maine
Maine Department of Health and Human Services
1-207-287-3707
http://www.maine.gov/dhhs

Maryland
Maryland Department of Human Resources
1-800-332-6347 or 1-410-767-7109
http://dhs.maryland.gov

Massachusetts
Massachusetts Department of Social Services
1-617-748-2000
http://www.mass.gov/dss
Massachusetts Executive Office of Health and Human Services
1-617-727-7600
http://www.mass.gov/eohhs

Michigan
Michigan Department of Community Health
1-517-373-3740
http://www.michigan.gov/mdch

Minnesota
Minnesota Department of Human Services
1-651-296-6117
http://www.dhs.state.mn.us

Mississippi
Mississippi Department of Human Services
1-800-345-6347
http://www.mdhs.ms.gov

Missouri
Missouri Department of Social Services
1-800-735-246 or 1-573-751-4815
http://www.dss.mo.gov

Montana
Montana Department of Public Health &; Human Services
1-406-444-5622
http://dphhs.mt.gov

Nebraska
Nebraska Health and Human Services System
1-402-471-9433
http://dhhs.ne.gov/Pages/default.aspx

Nevada
Nevada Department of Human Resources
1-775-687-4000
http://dhhs.nv.gov

New Hampshire
New Hampshire Department of Health and Human Services
1-603-271-4685
https://www.dhhs.nh.gov

New Jersey
New Jersey Department of Human Services
1-609-292-5325
http://www.state.nj.us/humanservices

New Mexico
New Mexico Human Services Department
1-355-827-7735
http://www.hsd.state.nm.us

New York
New York State Department of Health
1-518-474-5422
https://www.health.ny.gov

North Carolina
North Carolina Department of Health and Human Services

1-919-733-4534
https://www.ncdhhs.gov

North Dakota
North Dakota Department of Human Services
1-701-328-2310
http://www.nd.gov/humanservices

Pennsylvania
Pennsylvania Department of Human Services
1-800-692-7462
http://www.dhs.pa.gov

Rhode Island
Rhode Island Department of Human Services
1-401-462-2121
http://www.dhs.ri.gov

South Carolina
South Carolina Department of Health and Human Services
1-803-898-2350
https://www.scdhhs.gov

Tennessee
Tennessee Department of Human Services
1-615-313-4707
https://www.tn.gov/humanservices

Texas
Texas Health and Human Services Commission
1-800-252-8263
https://hhs.texas.gov

Utah
Utah Department of Health
1-801-538-6101
https://health.utah.gov

Vermont
Vermont Agency of Human Services
1-802-241-2220
http://humanservices.vermont.gov

Washington
Washington Department of Social and Health Services
1-360-902-7800
https://www.dshs.wa.gov

West Virginia
West Virginia Department of Health and Human Resources
1-304-558-0684
http://www.dhhr.wv.gov

Wisconsin
Wisconsin Department of Health and Family Services
1-608-266-9622
https://www.dhs.wisconsin.gov

Wyoming
Wyoming Department of Health
1-307-777-7656
https://health.wyo.gov

Notes

NOTES

Endnotes

Chapter 1

1. U.S. Bureau of the Census, "Older People Projected to Outnumber Children for First Time in U.S. History" (October 8, 2019), https://www.census.gov/newsroom/press-releases/2018/cb18-41-population-projections.html.

Chapter 2

2. U.S. Bureau of Labor Statistics, "Industries with the fastest growing and most rapidly declining wage and salary employment" (September 4, 2019), https://www.bls.gov/emp/tables/industries-fast-grow-decline-employment.htm.

3. Andrea M. Sisko and others, "National Health Expenditure Projections, 2018–27: Economic And Demographic Trends Drive Spending And Enrollment Growth," *Health Affairs* (February 20, 2019), https://www.healthaffairs.org/doi/10.1377/hlthaff.2018.05499.

4. "United States Home Care Market Report 2017-2024: Market was valued at $100 billion in 2016, and is projected to reach $225 billion - Research and Markets," *Business Wire*

(December 7, 2017), https://www.businesswire.com/news/home/20171207005595/en/United-States-Home-Care-Market-Report-2017-2024.

5. National Investment Center, "Property Market Size and Property Types of Seniors Housing & Care," https://www.nic.org/industry-resources/industry-faqs/property-market-size-property-types-seniors-housing-care.

6. U.S. Bureau of the Census, "By 2030, All Baby Boomers Will Be Age 65 or Older Population" (December 10, 2019), https://www.census.gov/library/stories/2019/12/by-2030-all-baby-boomers-will-be-age-65-or-older.html.

7. U.S. Bureau of the Census, "Older People Projected to Outnumber Children for First Time in U.S. History" (October 8, 2019), https://www.census.gov/newsroom/press-releases/2018/cb18-41-population-projections.html.

8. AARP, "Population Projections by Age, Sex, and Race/Ethnicity," (December 2013) https://dataexplorer.aarp.org/indicator/156/population-projections-by-age-sex-and-raceethnicity.

9. Suryatapa Bhattacharya, "In Fast-Aging Japan, Elder Care Is a High-Tech Pursuit," *Wall Street Journal* (January 12, 2019), https://www.wsj.com/articles/in-fast-aging-japan-elder-care-is-a-high-tech-pursuit-11547298000.

10. Malcolm Foster, "Aging Japan: Robots may have role in future of elder care," Reuters (March 27, 2018), https://www.reuters.com/article/us-japan-ageing-robots-widerimage/aging-japan-robots-may-have-role-in-future-of-elder-care-idUSKBN1H33AB.

11. ExpatFocus, "Italy - Elderly Care," https://www.expatfocus. com/italy/guide/elderly-care.

12. AARP, "The United States of Aging Survey — 2012," (June 6, 2012) https://web.archive.org/web/20140929125236/ https://www.aarp.org/content/dam/aarp/livable-communities/ learn/research/the-united-states-of-aging-survey-2012-aarp. pdf.

13. "2019 Axxess Staffing Survey," *Home Health Care News*, https://homehealthcarenews.com/hhcn-axxess-staffing-sur-vey/.

14. Metlife Mature Market Institute, "Miles Away: The Metlife Study of Long-Distance Caregiving" (July 2004), https://www. caregiving.org/data/milesaway.pdf.

15. National Association for Home Care & Hospice, "About NAHC," https://www.nahc.org/about.

16. Amy Baxter, "Longer Home Health Visits Tied to Lower Hospital Rates," *Home Health Care News* (May 14, 2018), https://homehealthcarenews.com/2018/05/longer-home-health-visits-tied-to-lower-hospital-rates.

17. William J. Freeman, Audrey J. Weiss, and Kevin C. Heslin, "Overview of U.S. Hospital Stays in 2016: Variation by Geographic Region," Healthcare Cost and Utilization Proj-ect (December 2018), https://www.hcup-us.ahrq.gov/reports/ statbriefs/sb246-Geographic-Variation-Hospital-Stays.jsp.

18. Tom Threlkeld, "Why Homecare Is the Answer to 2020's Big Health Care Questions," *HomeCare* (January 8, 2020), https://www.homecaremag.com/home-health-legislation-reg-ulation/why-homecare-answer-2020s-big-health-care-ques-tions.

19. Home Care Association of America and Global Coalition on Aging, "Caring for America's Seniors: The Value of Home Care," http://www.hcaoa.org/assets/1/27/Value_of_Home_Care___SECURED.pdf.

20. National Institute on Aging, "Alzheimer's Disease Fact Sheet" (May 22, 2019), https://www.nia.nih.gov/health/alzheimers-disease-fact-sheet.

21. Alzheimer's Association, "2019 Alzheimer's Disease Facts and Figures," https://www.alz.org/media/Documents/alzheimers-facts-and-figures-2019-r.pdf.

22. Ibid.

23. National Institutes of Health, "Parkinson's Disease Information Page," https://www.ninds.nih.gov/Disorders/All-Disorders/Parkinsons-Disease-Information-Page.

24. Parkinson's Foundation, "Stages of Parkinson's," https://www.parkinson.org/Understanding-Parkinsons/What-is-Parkinsons/Stages-of-Parkinsons.

25. Ibid.

26. Centers for Disease Control and Prevention, "Stroke Facts" (January 31, 2020), https://www.cdc.gov/stroke/facts.htm.

27. Ibid.

28. Ibid.

29. Johns Hopkins Medicine, "Effects of Stroke," https://www.hopkinsmedicine.org/health/conditions-and-diseases/stroke/effects-of-stroke.

30. American Stroke Foundation, "Preventing Another Stroke," https://www.stroke.org/en/life-after-stroke/preventing-another-stroke.

31. George Howard and David C. Goff, "Population shifts and the future of stroke: forecasts of the future burden of stroke," *Annals of the New York Academy of Sciences* (September 2012), https://www.ncbi.nlm.nih.gov/pmc/articles/PMC3727892/.

32. Rita R. Kalyani, Sherita H. Golden, and William T. Cefalu, "Diabetes and Aging: Unique Considerations and Goals of Care," *Diabetes Care* (April 2017), https://care.diabetesjournals.org/content/40/4/440.

33. National Institutes of Health, "Symptoms & Causes of Diabetes," https://www.niddk.nih.gov/health-information/diabetes/overview/symptoms-causes.

34. National Institutes of Health, "What is Diabetes?" https://www.niddk.nih.gov/health-information/diabetes/overview/what-is-diabetes.

35. National Institutes of Health, "Managing Diabetes," https://www.niddk.nih.gov/health-information/diabetes/overview/managing-diabetes.

36. Centers for Disease Control and Prevention, "Number of Americans with Diabetes Projected to Double or Triple by 2050" (October 22, 2010), https://www.cdc.gov/media/pressrel/2010/r101022.html.

Chapter 4

37. U.S. Small Business Administration, "Write your business plan," https://www.sba.gov/business-guide/plan-your-business/write-your-business-plan.

38. TJ McCue, "57 Million U.S. Workers Are Part of the Gig Economy," *Forbes* (August 31, 2018), https://www.forbes.

com/sites/tjmccue/2018/08/31/57-million-u-s-workers-are-part-of-the-gig-economy.

39. Internal Revenue Service, "Independent Contractor Defined," https://www.irs.gov/businesses/small-business-es-self-employed/independent-contractor-defined.

Chapter 5

40. Google, "General Guidelines," https://static.googleusercon-tent.com/media/guidelines.raterhub.com/en/searchqualit-yevaluatorguidelines.pdf.

41. Luke Harsel, "How to Write Killer Page Titles for SEO [Step-by-Step Guide]," *SEMrush Blog* (May 1, 2017), https://www.semrush.com/blog/on-page-seo-basics-page-titles.

42. Jay Peyton, "What's the Average Bounce Rate for a Website?" *RocketFuel*, https://www.gorocketfuel.com/the-rocket-blog/whats-the-average-bounce-rate-in-google-analytics.

Chapter 6

43. James C. Collins, *Good to Great: Why Some Companies Make the Leap … and Others Don't* (New York, NY: HarperBusiness, 2001). 164-188.

44. Robert Holly, "Word of Mouth Still Best Referral Source For Home Care Providers," *Home Health Care News*, (April 26, 2018), https://homehealthcarenews.com/2018/04/word-of-mouth-still-best-referral-source-for-home-care-providers.

Chapter 7

45. Craig Hales, Margaret D. Carroll, Cheryl D. Fryar, and Cynthia L. Ogden, "Prevalence of Obesity Among Adults and Youth: United States, 2015–2016" (NCHS Data Brief No.

288, October 2017), https://www.cdc.gov/nchs/products/databriefs/db288.htm.

46. Mark Mather, Linda A. Jacobsen, and Kelvin M. Pollard, "Population Bulletin" (Population Reference Bureau, December 2015), https://www.prb.org/wp-content/uploads/2016/01/aging-us-population-bulletin-1.pdf.

47. National Council on Aging, "Healthy Eating Tips for Seniors," https://www.ncoa.org/economic-security/benefits/food-and-nutrition/senior-nutrition.

48. Mayo Clinic, "Dehydration," https://www.mayoclinic.org/diseases-conditions/dehydration/symptoms-causes/syc-20354086.

49. Harvard Medical School, "5 medications that can cause problems in older age." *Harvard Health Letter* (August 2019), https://www.health.harvard.edu/staying-healthy/5-medications-that-can-cause-problems-in-older-age.

50. Ibid.

51. National Council on Aging, "Falls Prevention Facts," https://www.ncoa.org/news/resources-for-reporters/get-the-facts/falls-prevention-facts.

52. Marie-Christine Payette and others, "Fall-Related Psychological Concerns and Anxiety among Community-Dwelling Older Adults: Systematic Review and Meta-Analysis," *PLos One* (April 4, 2016), https://www.ncbi.nlm.nih.gov/pmc/articles/PMC4820267.

53. Julie Loebach Wetherell, "I'm very anxious about falling. What can I do?" Anxiety and Depression Association of America, https://adaa.org/living-with-anxiety/older-adults/fear-of-falling.

54. Nicole Ostrow, "Mobility Barriers' Impact on Daily Life of Patients With Knee Osteoarthritis," *Rheumatology Advisor* (July 14, 2017), https://www.rheumatologyadvisor.com/home/topics/osteoarthritis/mobility-barriers-impact-on-daily-life-of-patients-with-knee-osteoarthritis.

55. National Institutes of Health, "Social isolation, loneliness in older people pose health risks." (April 23, 2019), https://www.nia.nih.gov/news/social-isolation-loneliness-older-people-pose-health-risks.

56. Andrea L. Rosso, Loni P. Tabb, Tony H. Grubesic, Jennifer A. Taylor, and Yvonne L. Michael, "Neighborhood Social Capital and Achieved Mobility of Older Adults," *Journal of Aging and Health* (December 11, 2014), https://journals.sagepub.com/doi/abs/10.1177/0898264314523447.

Chapter 8

57. Paraprofessional Healthcare Institute, "U.S. Home Care Workers Key Facts" (August 2019), https://phinational.org/wp-content/uploads/2019/08/US-Home-Care-Workers-2019-PHI.pdf.

58. Ibid.

59. Stephen Campbell, "New Research: 7.8 Million Direct Care Jobs Will Need to Be Filled by 2026," Paraprofessional Healthcare Institute (January 24, 2019), https://phinational.org/news/new-research-7-8-million-direct-care-jobs-will-need-to-be-filled-by-2026.

60. Connor Kunz, "3 Key Takeaways From the 2019 Home Care Benchmarking Study," Rosemark (May 21, 2019), https://rosemarksystem.com/blog/3-key-takeaways-from-the-2019-home-care-benchmarking-study.

61. Misty Kempton, "How Much Is Caregiver Turnover Really Costing Your Business?" Home Care Pulse [AU: PLEASE ADD DATE IF POSSIBLE FOR CONSISTENCY], https://www.homecarepulse.com/articles/much-caregiver-turnover-really-costing-business.

62. Dennis Thompson, "Immigrants Make Up 1 in 4 U.S. Health Care Workers," *HealthDay* (June 3, 2019), https://consumer.healthday.com/caregiving-information-6/nursing-homes-and-elder-care-health-news-501/immigrants-make-up-1-in-4-u-s-health-care-workers-747081.html.

63. Connor Kutz, "The Ultimate Guide to Caregiver Recruitment," Home Care Pulse (September 19, 2018), https://www.homecarepulse.com/articles/ultimate-guide-caregiver-recruitment.

Chapter 9

64. Robyn I. Stone and Natasha S. Bryant, "The Future of the Home Care Workforce: Training and Supporting Aides as Members of Home-Based Care Teams." *Journal of the American Geriatrics Society* (May 10, 2019), https://onlinelibrary.wiley.com/doi/full/10.1111/jgs.15846.

65. Angelina Drake, "How 'Upskilling' Can Maximize Home Care Workers' Contributions and Improve Serious Illness Care," *Health Affairs* (March 4, 2019), https://www.healthaffairs.org/do/10.1377/hblog20190227.420595/full.

66. Paul Osterman, *Who Will Care for Us? Long-Term Care and the Long-Term Workforce* (Russell Sage Foundation, 2017), 10.

67. Family Caregiver Alliance, "Caregiver Statistics: Demographics," https://www.caregiver.org/caregiver-statistics-de-

mographics.

68. Courtney E. Martin, "A New Wave of Caregivers: Men," *The New York Times* (September 18, 2019), https://www.nytimes.com/2019/09/18/opinion/male-care-giver.html.

69. Zack Friedman, "Student Loan Debt Statistics In 2020: A Record $1.6 Trillion," *Forbes* (February 3, 2020), https://www.forbes.com/sites/zackfriedman/2020/02/03/student-loan-debt-statistics.

70. Lanekassen, "Regulations regarding interest on and payment of educational loans and loss of rights" (2016), https://www.lanekassen.no/Global/Forskrifter/2016/Repayment%20rules%202016_EN.pdf.

71. Robert Farrington, "The Guide to Temporary Expanded Public Service Loan Forgiveness," *The College Investor*, (February 11, 2020), https://thecollegeinvestor.com/24410/temporary-expanded-public-service-loan-forgiveness.

72. Zack Friedman, "Student Loan Debt Statistics In 2020: A Record $1.6 Trillion," *Forbes* (February 3, 2020), https://www.forbes.com/sites/zackfriedman/2020/02/03/student-loan-debt-statistics.

73. Kevin Payne,"How to Know If Teacher Loan Forgiveness Is Worth It," *Student Loan Planner* (September 19, 2019), https://www.studentloanplanner.com/teacher-loan-forgiveness-student-loans-worth-it.

74. Nimrod Kaplan, "Smart Sensors Can Help Seniors Age In Place," *Forbes* (September 5, 2018), https://www.forbes.com/sites/forbestechcouncil/2018/09/05/smart-sensors-can-help-seniors-age-in-place.

75. Ibid.

76. Heartline, "About the Heartline Study," https://www.heart-line.com/about.

77. Brenda Rudman, "Art Without Boundaries: A Brush with Success," *SignPost* (April 25, 2011), https://web.archive.org/web/20110425073016/http:/artwithoutboundaries.net/SignpostArticle.html.

78. Johns Hopkins School of Nursing, "Community Aging in Place—Advancing Better Living for Elders (CAPABLE)," https://nursing.jhu.edu/faculty_research/research/projects/capable.

79. Ibid.

CPSIA information can be obtained
at www.ICGtesting.com
Printed in the USA
BVHW040903250720
584552BV00007B/21